'I have enjoyed Michael Neill's work for many years and benefited from it in my own life. In **The Inside-Out Revolution**, he offers a brilliant approach for creating more peace of mind while keeping your edge in today's busy world. Don't just read this book – let it pour into your consciousness and revolutionize your life!'
PAUL MCKENNA, INTERNATIONAL BESTSELLING AUTHOR OF *CHANGE YOUR LIFE IN 7 DAYS* AND *I CAN MAKE YOU THIN*

'I did not expect to read this in one sitting, but once I started I couldn't stop. **The Inside-Out Revolution** encompasses the beauty and wisdom of the ages, delivered in a way that makes it extremely relevant to today's challenges. Michael Neill writes not as a guru or an expert, but as a friend who has found the way home and is eager to share the path with the reader. If you could only read one book in your lifetime, I'd recommend this one.'
SHAMA KABANI, CEO OF THE MARKETING ZEN GROUP

'**The Inside-Out Revolution** is a powerful new way to wake ourselves up out of the trance of life. Destined to be a practical, spiritual classic, this book shows you exactly how your thoughts create your reality.'
GAY HENDRICKS, PH.D., NEW YORK TIMES BESTSELLING AUTHOR OF *CONSCIOUS LOVING* AND THE *TENZING NORBU MYSTERIES*

'Truly revolutionary – the most profound and life-changing message you will ever read. This is a book you'll pick up time and again – I've read it three times and am already recommending it to all the students I teach and individuals I coach.'
JANE HOLROYD MBE, VISITING FELLOW, BOURNEMOUTH UNIVERSITY

'**The Inside-Out Revolution** is simply a beautiful presentation of the only thing you need to know for well-being and happiness. Written from personal insights and real-life examples, Michael Neill makes it easy to grasp the innate principles that create our feelings and experience. I highly recommend this book to anyone wanting true wisdom.'
MARK HOWARD, PH.D., CLINICAL PSYCHOLOGIST, THREE PRINCIPLES INSTITUTE

'I love this book! What Michael Neill shares so eloquently is at the heart of what Richard and I learned, taught, and wrote about throughout our lives together – a true understanding of mental health and how to access it quickly and effectively for a better life.'
KRISTINE CARLSON, CO-AUTHOR WITH RICHARD CARLSON TO THE NEW YORK TIMES BESTSELLING *DON'T SWEAT THE SMALL STUFF* BOOK SERIES

'One day, every school will have a class on teaching children how to think. Michael Neill's brilliant new book **The Inside-Out Revolution** *will be both the handbook that teachers read for prep and the primer for the class.'*
ROBERT HOLDEN PH.D., BESTSELLING AUTHOR OF *SHIFT HAPPENS!* AND *LOVEABILITY*

'Camera, sound, ACTION! Michael's new book has thoughtful and practical "rubber-to-the-road" steps to clear your mind and to actually start living a simple and more relaxed life.'
ANDREW LITVIN, OSCAR AND BAFTA AWARD-WINNING LINE PRODUCER AND PRODUCER OF *GINGER & ROSA*

'In **The Inside-Out Revolution**, *Michael Neill has beautifully captured the essence of the three universal principles at the source of human experience. This book will be a powerful change agent in creating a more gentle, loving, creative, productive, and peaceful world.'*
DR. WILLIAM F. PETTIT JR., FORMER ASSOCIATE PROFESSOR OF PSYCHIATRY, UNIVERSITY OF WEST VIRGINIA

'Michael Neill has the rare gift of enabling people to make tangible changes without hard work or struggle. In **The Inside-Out Revolution**, *he offers a clear, practical way of understanding life to create a more peaceful and fluid way of living.'*
SHAA WASMUND, FOUNDER OF SMARTA.COM AND NO. 1 BESTSELLING AUTHOR OF *STOP TALKING, START DOING*

'Living from the inside-out isn't just a revolutionary concept – it's a truth about the way life works. If you've spent your life looking for answers, get ready for a miracle – this book provides the one answer in life that's been looking for you. Sit back, take your time, and absorb.'
GARRET KRAMER, AUTHOR OF *STILLPOWER: EXCELLENCE WITH EASE IN SPORTS AND LIFE*

'Michael Neill's authentic, conversational style profoundly and simply describes a quiet revolution happening in psychology that recognizes the human experience is created from the inside out. **The Inside-Out Revolution** is a great book – excellent, articulate, and an apt harbinger of the paradigmatic shift that is to come.'
JOSEPH BAILEY, LICENSED PSYCHOLOGIST AND INTERNATIONAL BESTSELLING AUTHOR OF *SLOWING DOWN TO THE SPEED OF LIFE*, CO-AUTHORED BY DR. RICHARD CARLSON

'I cried the first time I read **The Inside-Out Revolution** and then I read it again and made notes on every page. If you have eyes to see and ears to hear, this book will set you free.'
STEVE HARDISON, WWW.THEULTIMATECOACH.COM

'Michael Neill's new book elegantly translates his deep, compelling understanding of the human condition into an inspirational, high-impact teaching. This book is an invitation to experience a clarity that will transform your life forever!'
DR. THOMAS GARTENMANN, MANAGING DIRECTOR, MANRES AG – LEADING TRANSFORMATION, ZURICH-COLOGNE

'Michael has a unique gift for making the impossibly complicated incredibly simple – his teaching is like a force of nature with a simple grace and flow that packs incredible power for those who let it into their lives. **The Inside-Out Revolution** is not just a new book, it's a new way of living that will transform the quality of your life faster, easier, and much more gently than you think.'
ALI CAMPBELL, BESTSELLING AUTHOR AND CELEBRITY LIFE COACH

'Michael Neill has done it again – here's a blueprint for a truly wonderful life, based on a new way of looking, knowing, and being. **The Inside-Out Revolution** is a brave and compelling perspective, easily understood and implemented. Go beyond techniques and strategies, and watch what changes for you when you experience life from the inside out. Highly recommended.'
CHRIS WESTFALL, NATIONAL ELEVATOR PITCH CHAMPION (USA) AND AUTHOR OF *THE NEW ELEVATOR PITCH*

'Rarely does a book make such a poetic and exciting series of promises and then deliver on all of them. This one does, and it will change lives.'
STEVE CHANDLER, AUTHOR OF *TIME WARRIOR* AND *100 WAYS TO MOTIVATE YOURSELF*

'When Michael Neill and I first had a conversation about the principles he shares in this book, they seemed too simple to make a big difference. But the more I explored them, the more I realized that their very simplicity was the source of their power. When you read **The Inside-Out Revolution**, Michael has that conversation with you. Get ready to discover a place of profound peace: your unique source of guidance, life-changing insights, and creative solutions. Highly recommended!'

JAMIE SMART, AUTHOR OF CLARITY: CLEAR MIND, BETTER PERFORMANCE, BIGGER RESULTS

'This is not a book about doing; it is a book about being. And it doesn't just talk about transformation – it transforms you as you read it. I felt things that had been big issues simply become laughable, and found myself growing more peaceful, happy, and joyful with every chapter!'

STEVER ROBBINS, CO-FOUNDER OF FTP SOFTWARE AND HOST OF NO. 1 ITUNES BUSINESS PODCAST THE GET-IT-DONE GUY

'I have used the principles in **The Inside-Out Revolution** to run two international consultancies and have taught them to Generals, CEO's, and numerous Fortune 500 companies. Michael Neill's new book introduces these principles in a wonderfully simple and relevant way while using them to provide a powerful new foundation for coaching, self-development and the pursuit of happiness. All that and an enjoyable read as well.'

AARON TURNER, PH.D., CO-FOUNDER/SENIOR PARTNER TURNER GLEASON

'In my work in hospitals, I witness people suffering and in pain every single day. As I read **The Inside-Out Revolution**, I could clearly see how an end to human suffering is possible, not by changing the world but through a deeper understanding of ourselves. This is the first and last book you will ever need to read to understand how to live a happy, inspired love-filled life.'

FIONA JACOB, DIRECTOR OF NURSING, KING ABDULAZIZ MEDICAL CITY, RIYADH

'This book has the power to create miracles in our lives as we come to recognize our true inner majesty and release our incredible power to shape our world.'

DAVID R. HAMILTON PH.D., AUTHOR OF IS YOUR LIFE MAPPED OUT? AND HOW YOUR MIND CAN HEAL YOUR BODY

THE
INSIDE
OUT
REVOLUTION

THE
INSIDE
OUT
REVOLUTION

THE ONLY THING YOU
NEED TO KNOW TO CHANGE
YOUR LIFE FOREVER

MICHAEL NEILL

HAY HOUSE

Carlsbad, California • New York City • London • Sydney
Johannesburg • Vancouver • Hong Kong • New Delhi

First published and distributed in the United Kingdom by:
Hay House UK Ltd, Astley House, 33 Notting Hill Gate, London W11 3JQ
Tel: +44 (0)20 3675 2450; Fax: +44 (0)20 3675 2451
www.hayhouse.co.uk

Published and distributed in the United States of America by:
Hay House Inc., PO Box 5100, Carlsbad, CA 92018-5100
Tel: (1) 760 431 7695 or (800) 654 5126
Fax: (1) 760 431 6948 or (800) 650 5115
www.hayhouse.com

Published and distributed in Australia by:
Hay House Australia Ltd, 18/36 Ralph St, Alexandria NSW 2015
Tel: (61) 2 9669 4299; Fax: (61) 2 9669 4144
www.hayhouse.com.au

Published and distributed in the Republic of South Africa by:
Hay House SA (Pty) Ltd, PO Box 990, Witkoppen 2068
Tel/Fax: (27) 11 467 8904
www.hayhouse.co.za

Published and distributed in India by:
Hay House Publishers India, Muskaan Complex, Plot No.3, B-2,
Vasant Kunj, New Delhi 110 070
Tel: (91) 11 4176 1620; Fax: (91) 11 4176 1630
www.hayhouse.co.in

Distributed in Canada by:
Raincoast, 9050 Shaughnessy St, Vancouver BC V6P 6E5
Tel: (1) 604 323 7100; Fax: (1) 604 323 2600

A catalogue record for this book is available from the British Library.

ISBN: 978-1-78180-079-9

Image p.46 © ScienceCartoonsPlus.com

Printed and bound in Great Britain by TJ International Ltd.

MIX
Paper from
responsible sources
FSC
www.fsc.org   FSC® C013056

To Nina, for everything and always

'If the only thing people learned was not to be afraid of their experience, that alone would change the world.'

SYD BANKS

CONTENTS

FOREWORD

Thirty years ago, I met a man named Sydney Banks and became the co-founder of a new paradigm in psychology that has since quietly spread throughout the world. Up to now this approach, as life-changing as it has been, has been an extremely well-kept secret. In this new book, Michael Neill brings the principles behind this field into the mainstream so that people can learn to take advantage of this radical new understanding in their own lives. His target audience: anybody, no matter what their walk in life and no matter how happy or troubled they are right now. It's simply a 'good-for-what-ails-you' book in terms of internal well-being and effective performance.

Everyone feels limited and constricted by negative feeling states more than they would like to be. We all visit, and at times seem to live in, unwanted feelings of stress and distress that cast the die regarding our enjoyment of life, our performance on the job, and the quality of our relationships. Any good sales manager will tell you that the number one obstacle to sales performance is an ongoing feeling of discouragement; any experienced therapist will point out that feelings of hopelessness sap people's energy, undermine their judgment, and lead to the downward spiral of depression. It should resonate as self-evident that chronic negative feeling states restrict the human potential.

But the opposite is also true. Everyone experiences times of mental clarity and well-being, even moments of out and out genius. Even in the extremes of mental illness, every single patient has moments of 'normalcy' independent of the severity of their disorder. At a more personal level, we have all come up with inspirations and solutions that seem to have shown up out of nowhere to save the day. At times, our children's wisdom goes way beyond their level of education and life experience. And we consistently see high levels of well-being, grace, and hopefulness emerge in times of crisis such as floods and earthquakes, and even with people informed of terminal illnesses. So it should be equally obvious that the human potential for life enjoyment, mental clarity, creativity, and relationship satisfaction is considerably higher than we are manifesting in our everyday lives. What that potential is, where it comes from, and how to tap into it are the questions Michael Neill answers in this book.

The current thinking offers a laundry list of explanations for why people feel and behave the way they do, ranging from genetics and family of origin conditioning to childhood trauma, challenging life circumstances, and even the weather. Each of these explanations is plagued by exceptions and anomalies, and, perhaps more importantly, none of them significantly help people to improve their habitual personal feeling state, or lead to consistent improvements in behavior.

By way of contrast, the principles Michael presents in this book provide an explanation of the human experience and feeling states that is comprehensive, has no exceptions, and is extremely useful to nearly everyone who learns about them. You won't find the principles he teaches here anywhere else in psychology, the media, or the self-help world. In fact, the only people who are sharing the understanding that he presents here got it from the same source. It is simply a new and enlightened understanding of where human experience comes from and how it can be changed for the better without any techniques, strategies, or prescribed behaviors.

This alone would make this book worth reading, no matter how it was expressed, but fortunately Michael is a very gifted writer. He writes in a very conversational, personable tone, as if you were sitting in his living room and listening to him share some ideas and stories. And I encourage you to read this book in that way. Don't try too hard to understand everything first time around. Listen to his message the way you might listen to a piece of music, enjoying the theme and letting it wash over you.

I know first-hand that anybody who grasps the teachings in this book will experience an immediate improvement in their level of well-being, no matter how well they're feeling at present. They will perform better in their lives and appreciate the fruits of their labor more than they ever have before.

No matter where you're starting out, all boats rise with the tide, and a deeper understanding of the principles in this book will improve your life across the board. You will think with more clarity, be more resilient (get over yourself faster when you're troubled), be significantly more creative, and be immune from burnout on a go forward basis.

I realize that these claims might seem like hyperbole, but in over 30 years of teaching what Michael is sharing here, I have seen these results so consistently that I am no longer surprised or even impressed. In short, this book is the real deal.

George Pransky, Ph.D.
La Conner, Washington

INTRODUCTION:
A PERSONAL REVOLUTION

What if everything you'd ever learned about how reality worked was just wrong?

In 2007, I thought I was at the top of my game. My coaching practice was thriving, I was well respected in my particular field of applied psychology, my first book had been a bestseller, and my second book was just about to come out in America. My wife, Nina, and I were in our twentieth year together and our three kids were everything we could have hoped for and more.

About the only difficulty I had in my life was that Nina and I were in the middle of an ongoing debate about whether or not we should move to a new house. It was certainly what might be called a 'high-quality problem,' but that didn't stop me from complaining about it to anyone who would listen.

A friend of mine grew tired of my whining and sent me a copy of *The Relationship Handbook* by Dr. George Pransky, which I fully intended to ignore completely. I'm not a fan of relationship books at the best of times, as I find they're generally filled with wonderful advice which works great if you happen to be the author. But I opened the book to read the first chapter and became fascinated by Dr. Pransky's descriptions of 'high mood therapy' and 'maintenance-free relationships.'

By the end of the day I'd read the whole book and resolved to be more open-minded the next time someone suggested I read something that might be good for me.

I thought no more about it until my friend asked how things were going with Nina.

I said, 'What do you mean?'

'Well, how are you getting on?'

'Great. Why do you ask?'

It took him a half-dozen more questions before I remembered that less than a week earlier we'd been in the thick of one of the worst arguments we'd had in years. At that moment, I felt a cold shiver up the back of my spine. Something in that book had led to amnesia about the biggest problem I'd thought I had. To my surprise, even after I remembered it, I couldn't get worked up about it anymore. Oddly, it seemed to stop being a big problem for

Nina as well, without our even talking about it. The house situation wound up resolving itself in due course, and I was hooked. I needed to learn more.

CURIOUSER AND CURIOUSER

When I went online to do some research about the basis for the book, I was amazed to find scattered artifacts of a field of psychology that was new to me. It had begun appearing in the literature in the late 1970s under an eclectic set of names, ranging from 'Psychology of Mind' to 'Health Realization' to 'The Three Principles.' Richard Carlson, author of the bestselling *Don't Sweat the Small Stuff* series, had been by far its most famous practitioner, but as far as I could tell he'd drifted away from the community around the time he'd started to become successful.

As I looked into it more deeply, I discovered that the primary influence behind the field was a Scottish welder named Syd Banks, who had had an enlightenment experience and been transformed from an uneducated worker in a Canadian pulp mill into a world-renowned guru and teacher. Everyone I spoke with in the field had a story about how meeting Syd or reading his books had been a transformative moment in their life, and I grew more and more intrigued by the fact that despite nearly 20 years of studying psychology and personal development, I'd never heard of him or the fields he'd inspired.

To make matters even more confusing, each person I spoke with confided that there was no 'technique' behind their transformation – you simply listened to Syd or one of the people trained in his work speak about three simple principles, and at some point a transformation happened and your life was never the same again.

The list of claims made by practitioners in the field beggared belief. Former gang members became positive role models within their communities. Alcoholics kicked their addiction without years of struggle or therapy. Two housing projects with the highest murder rates in America became crime free within three years of the residents being exposed to these principles.

I spoke with a CEO who had taken his company from millions to billions of dollars in revenue by teaching the inside-out understanding to his workforce and letting the numbers take care of themselves. And unlike the 'experts' in most other fields of psychology I'd come across, nearly everyone I met with was happily married, had good relationships with their children, and was still inspired by their work after more than 30 years in the field.

I decided that I needed to abandon objectivity and flew out to a small town near the Canadian border to explore this approach for myself.

What I experienced there turned my life inside out, my career upside-down, and changed the way I saw the world.

And it all came about not through a special technique or magic pill, but simply through participating in a very particular kind of conversation. That conversation is now the basis of all the work I do with my clients, and it's the conversation that you and I will be having together over the course of this book.

A PREVIEW OF COMING ATTRACTIONS

During our time together, I'll be sharing a new understanding that turns most of psychology on its head. By recognizing three fundamental principles at play behind every human experience, it becomes possible to tap into a deeper intelligence behind life that informs our mental health, supplies us with ongoing wisdom and guidance, and allows us to unleash incredible creative power into the world. We'll look at making a return to 'original grace,' and explore how the inside-out understanding allows us to handle life's challenges with ease and power, play the game of life full out and fearless, and go beyond empowerment to find our place in the larger unfolding of the world.

Since stumbling across this revolutionary new understanding in my own life, I've introduced it to thousands of people around the world and personally coached hundreds to shift their foundations, learn how to thrive, and live from the inside out. My clients and students have made positive and sometimes dramatic changes in their relationships, finances, mental and physical health, and well-being. They've become happier, more secure in themselves, and more compassionate with others.

But many of them have also come face to face with challenging circumstances. Some of them have lost their jobs, gone bankrupt, become ill, and dealt with family crises that bring tears to my eyes just thinking about them. Almost without fail, they've found deep reserves of resilience and creativity that have allowed them to handle these difficult circumstances with a level of ease and grace they would previously never have imagined possible.

If you were to talk with them, you'd find them to be as different from one another as people can be – male and female, young and old, rich and poor. But from the time they had the inside-out understanding for themselves, chances are you'd notice two things they all had in common: a twinkle in their eye and a lovely feeling in their presence.

Some people describe this transformative shift as moving from riding a roller coaster to floating in a river; others as the gift of meeting themselves for the first time. 'It's as if I've been plugged back into the mains,' one client said to me. By far the most common description is some variation on the feeling of coming home after a long time away. While your experience will be unique to you, the awakening of your inner spark and a feeling of reconnection with the energy of life are part of the promise and purpose of our time together.

While the nature of a book is that I'll be doing most of the talking, your job is equally important – to listen with an open mind, do your best to look in the direction I'm pointing, and above all to stay in the conversation to the very end. In fact, the only way I know for someone not to get something of value from this conversation is to drop out of it before they've seen what there is to see on the other side of the rainbow.

There are no techniques anywhere in this book – there's nothing for you to learn, remember, practice, or do. I'm simply going to point us toward some fundamental truths about life and we'll see what we can see. Sometimes it may feel as though we're getting nowhere, or even going backward. Other times new insights will be coming through you so quickly that you may struggle to keep up.

But if you keep reading with an open mind and a hopeful heart, I promise you that your life will not only change for the better, it will also begin to impact the lives of those around you in ways that you can only now imagine.

Here's a letter I received from a young woman who participated in my *Living from the Inside Out* online program at a time when her life circumstances couldn't have been much worse:

'When I first learned about the principles behind the inside-out understanding, I was looking into ways of how I could go about ending my life. Within just a few *short days, through your teaching, I had gained so much clarity and peace. Inspiration came to me and where I thought that I would never experience feelings of love ever again, my whole being became love, and vibrant.*

I find myself living in a state of tranquility, despite some quite difficult circumstances. I face arguments with gentleness and give my replies directly from my inner sense of well-being. Because I am no longer trapped in my own thinking, I can look inside other people and see how they're feeling. It's almost as if this has opened up some kind of sixth sense.

I see the world with renewed sight, not all day every day, but almost.

And best of all, these simple ideas have allowed me to tap into who I really am, so that no matter what happens around me, I always have that security and sense of freedom. It may waver at times but it always comes back. And I am a person who no longer looks into ways of how I can end my life.'

What allowed her to experience that kind of clarity, peace, and freedom in the middle of her worst nightmare is what we'll be exploring together in this book.

Are you ready to begin?

1

SHIFTING THE FOUNDATIONS

'Reality is an illusion, albeit an extremely persistent one.'

THE TRANSFORMATIVE CONVERSATION

*'We have the most wonderful job in the world.
We find people in various stages of sleep.
And then we get to tap them on the shoulder
and be with them as they wake up to the full
magnificence of life.'*

Syd Banks

Imagine that a man comes to you for coaching. He's about to turn 30 and he's decided that it's time to 'grow up' and take over the family carpentry business. He wants you to share innovative marketing techniques, work with him on how to make better personnel decisions, and coach him to incorporate technology to bring the business into 'at least the new millennium.'

But even as you're speaking together, something's bothering you about the conversation. He's saying all the right things and seems willing to do all the right things, and yet something still feels out of alignment. Following your intuition, you go back and review the client intake form he filled out when he first came to you, and to your surprise you see that his name is Jesus and he's from a small town in the Galilean region of Israel called Nazareth.

Here's the question:

Do you really want to work with him on becoming more successful in his carpentry business?

What if every man, woman, and child you meet has the seeds within them to become who they truly are?

What if that includes you?

GOING DEEPER

When people ask me to tell them more about the transformative conversation, I tend to explain it like this:

'It's a meaningful conversation about the nature of the human experience.'

When we look to the 'nature' of something, we're looking to see it not as it appears through our own eyes but as it is before being seen. Or, to put it in considerably simpler terms, we're looking to see the truth of it, even as we recognize the inevitability of distorting that truth the moment we attempt to describe it in words. And the deeper we look in the direction of the truth behind the human experience, the more we're likely to see.

We seem to have an innate desire to know ourselves at deeper and deeper levels. For most of us, this journey begins with an exploration of our own individual psychology. This kind of self-analysis can reveal an extraordinary amount of data and distinctions, as we discover we're introverted or extroverted, have high or low self-esteem, and are more or less honest with ourselves than we'd hoped or feared.

But self-awareness can quickly turn to self-consciousness, as each new observation is coupled with a judgment and an attempt to fix our 'faults' and improve our 'virtues.' Before long, we become hopelessly entangled in a struggle against our own psyche, spending countless hours and endless effort trying to 'become the person we think we ought to be.'

By way of contrast, when we look away from our own unique peccadilloes and consider the nature of the *human* experience, we discover a very interesting thing: that most of what we thought was wrong with us is simply a part of the human condition.

Everybody has moods. Everybody does things that seem like a good idea at the time and then regrets them later. Everybody fails at some things and succeeds at others, and the ratio is usually more a function of what they choose to attempt than any personal genius or lack of potential.

When we stop asking, 'What's true about me?' and begin asking, 'What's true about human beings in general?' we discover things about our incredible capacity for resilience, creativity and hope. People are amazing – a fact that's much easier to see when we aren't looking at 'them' in some kind of judgmental comparison with 'us.'

The *human experience* is that which is true for all human beings. So, when I speak with people, we begin by having a conversation about some aspect of their life – money, career, performance, relationships, etc. – and it inevitably evolves into a conversation about the nature of life in general. And as a result of that conversation, their lives transform.

Now I know that sounds like a big promise to make, but I've seen it happen so many times that I no longer shy away from saying it. When people see something fundamental about the nature of their experience, their relationship to that experience shifts. And as a result of that shift, life begins to change, seemingly without effort – all by itself.

ELEMENTS OF TRANSFORMATION

There are two elements that always seem to be present in any genuinely transformative conversation. The first is what I would call 'a deeper feeling.' Describing what exactly this is like has been both the inspiration and bane of every spiritual teacher throughout the ages. I imagine it's like trying to describe a sunset to a blind person – you can be accurate down to the tiniest detail, but no matter how close you get, it's still a million miles away from the real thing. Over the years, I've heard the world of deeper feeling inside us called everything from 'the unconditioned mind' to 'nirvana' to 'innate mental health' and 'innate well-being.' I call it 'the space where miracles happen.' And I've discovered that, like many things worth having, it seems to run away the moment you begin chasing it.

It's not that it really goes anywhere; it's just that when the thoughts in our head get revved up, they seem so much more important and real than something as 'trivial' as a deeper feeling. This has been true in my own life to the point where at times I've chalked all my experiences of that deeper feeling up to imagination and self-delusion. Yet the moment I drop back into it, I know the exact opposite to be true. My thoughts are clearly the impostors, creating the illusion of reality all around me while the truth is right here inside.

In the transformative conversation, we slow things down enough to notice that this world of deeper feeling is always available to us. It becomes both our companion and our guide, keeping us warm in the midst of cold circumstances, lending fire to our own inspiration, and letting us know when we're on or off track by its presence or absence.

The second thing that all truly transformative conversations seem to have in common is that instead of looking at the details of our life to make sense of our experience, they direct us inward toward the source and nature of that experience.

By way of example, I had a conversation with a client recently who was going through a difficult divorce. When I asked her how it was all unfolding, she said that despite a delay in the proceedings, things had been 'very up and down.'

I then asked her what she made of the fact that her experience was fluctuating much more quickly than her circumstances were changing.

This led us into a beautiful exploration of how experience always follows thought, regardless of what's going on around us. She got quiet and, as almost inevitably happens, she was struck by an insight that left her feeling much stronger and more capable than before. She expressed her gratitude for all the things in her life that were still wonderful, including her relationships with her children and her relative state of well-being considering everything she was going through.

Because she was able to see that her experience was being created from the inside out, she was less frightened of what might happen next – which gave her immediate access to the resources and common sense we all have to guide us when we're on our game.

Will she lose her bearings again and have more 'up and down' weeks? Of course she will. But each time it happens it will be easier for her to see that all that's going on is some insecure thinking, and that the moment it passes, what to do – if there's anything to be done – will once again become clear.

And this is the gift of a deeper understanding: it frees us from having to try to control our experience, avoid anything we don't want to have happen or never feel down again. With that freedom comes so much energy and lightness that we reconnect to the world of deeper feeling. And life once again feels like the gift it was always meant to be.

DANCING BETWEEN THE SPIRITUAL AND THE MATERIAL

At the physicist David Bohm's funeral, one of his favorite passages from his own work was read aloud:

> *The field of the finite is all that we can see, hear, touch, remember, and describe. This field is basically that which is manifest, or tangible.*

> *The essential quality of the infinite, by contrast, is its subtlety, its intangibility. This quality is conveyed in the word 'spirit,' whose root meaning is 'wind or breath.' This suggests an invisible but pervasive energy, to which the manifest world of the finite responds.*

> *This energy, or spirit, infuses all living things, and without it any organism must fall apart into its constituent elements. That which is truly alive in living*

*systems is this energy of spirit, and this is never born
and never dies.*

In other words, we live in a world of spirit (the infinite)
made manifest in a world of form (the finite). Which means
that everything is made of spirit and nothing (literally 'no
thing') is the essence of spirit.

In the same way, the transformative conversation is, by
nature, both psychological and spiritual. After all, if we're
to look more deeply into what it is to be alive, aware,
and creative, we must consider both the workings of
the human mind and the larger context in which we as
human beings function.

The French Jesuit Teilhard de Chardin famously said, 'We
are not human beings having a spiritual experience – we
are spiritual beings having a human experience.' And if this
is true, we ignore either of those facts at our peril.

People who attempt to live purely in the material world
and ignore the spiritual tend, in my experience, to ride the
roller coaster of life's ups and downs and arrive at the end
of the ride feeling – accurately – that they haven't actually
gotten anywhere and wondering why those spiritual people
seem so calm and peaceful.

People who emphasize the spiritual world at the cost of
the material tend, in my experience, to fluctuate between
moments of pure bliss/awe/wonder and moments of
frustration, wondering why, if they're so spiritual, God/

Life/the Universe has forsaken them to a life of poverty and struggle while those material people get to have all the nice stuff.

To attempt to choose between the spiritual and the material is like trying to choose between two cars, one without an engine and one without a steering wheel – you won't be arriving anywhere worthwhile in either of them.

This isn't to say we need to attempt to balance the two – worship on the weekends and work in the week is more of a cultural norm than a life strategy. But when we begin to see how the two worlds are really one, it becomes possible to experience the best of both.

The upside of a focus on the spiritual is a deeper sense of connection with ourselves, with others, and with life itself. The world of deeper feelings that we begin to inhabit – feelings like gratitude, love, humility, wonder, and awe is its own reward.

The upside of a focus on the material is a life of greater comfort, ease, and possibility. Money may not be able to buy happiness or love, but it's the best tool I know for feeding children, building new homes, buying plane tickets to a tropical island, and having a romantic dinner for two on the beach once you're there.

The difficulty comes if we start to treat the formless world of spirit as if it's subject to the same rules as the world of form. Most of us are familiar with what happens when we're consumed with the pursuit of success in the material world. Stress and pressure become our constant companions, and more is somehow not only better but also never enough. If we win the game, our ex-husbands, wives, and children get to read our epitaph in the morning headlines:

'Here lies the fastest runner on the treadmill.'

If we approach the world of spirit in the same way, we set ourselves up for yet another lifetime of struggle. We strive for 'spiritual success,' setting enlightenment or union with the divine as our goal and determining that we will out-meditate, out-pray, and outlast our fellow seekers until we get voted 'most likely to sit at the right hand of God' in our high-school yearbooks.

In both cases, our endless pursuit of 'not this' is driven by our deepest fear: that there's something wrong with us and we're not enough. That until we achieve sufficient levels of spiritual wealth, material success, or both, we won't be worthy of love. And that without something tangible to show for it, we'll have wasted our life.

Ironically, what we're seeking is all around us all the time. Right where you're sitting now is the infinite whole made manifest in the divine specific. You could no sooner be 'not enough' than a tree could be the wrong color. And you don't have to become worthy of love, because love is what you're made of.

When we see that truth, or indeed any truth about the human condition, it can set us free. There are millions of theories out there, and I've added a few dozen of my own to the list over the years. But, as Syd Banks used to say:

'You only need to see one spiritual fact
and it will change your life forever.'

PUTTING IT ALL TOGETHER

In the next chapter I'm going to be sharing three spiritual facts — three 'principles,' or foundational elements, of the human experience. But before we move forward, here are a few of the key insights from this chapter to reflect upon:

▶ We cannot even begin to guess at the full scope of the human potential, including our own.

▶ What is truly transformative is seeing what's still there even when we're not looking.

▶ There is a world of deeper feeling which is always available to us.

▶ If we are truly spiritual beings having a human experience, we ignore either of those facts at our peril.

▶ We don't have to become worthy of love, because love is what we're made of.

▶ You only need to see one spiritual fact to change your life forever.

FIRST PRINCIPLES

*'In every systematic inquiry (**methodos**)*
where there are first principles, or causes, or
elements, knowledge and science result from
acquiring knowledge of these... It is clear, then,
that in the science of nature as elsewhere, we
should try first to determine questions about
the first principles.'

Aristotle

There are usually only a few basic principles that form the basis for our understanding of anything in life. When we get really clear on what those principles are, we've got the key to unlocking the mystery of whatever that thing is. And once we've unlocked those mysteries, they cease to be mysteries – the inquiry opens doors that never become closed to us again.

One of the fundamental principles in geometry is what's called the 'point-line-plane postulate.' There's no such thing in nature as a point, but if we accept the idea of a point as a first principle, we can then put an infinite sequence of points together and get a line. And if we envision a series of lines going in every direction in a single dimension (like an endless piece of paper), we get a plane.

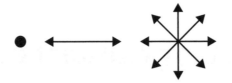

By asserting these three fundamental principles and then building on them, everything else in geometry and design becomes possible, from creating shapes to designing buildings.

Or think about another kind of plane – the kind that flies over our head all day long. Until about 100 years ago, flight seemed impossible to most scientists, even though it was happening all around them in nature. Then a couple of brothers who ran a bike shop figured out a way to take some fundamental principles – like gravity, lift, thrust, and drag – and combine them in a new way to enable something heavy to behave as if it were lighter than air.

So the word 'principle,' as I'll be using it in our conversation together, refers to the basic or essential quality or element of something that determines its intrinsic nature or characteristic behavior.

In the field of chemistry, 117 distinct elements have been discovered that in various compounds form the substance of every 'thing' on the planet. In art, the three primary colors make up every other color in the spectrum.

When Syd Banks began talking about his insights into the human experience, he articulated their essence in the form of three universal principles, which he called *Mind*, *Consciousness*, and *Thought*. While those words mean different things to different people, the principles they point to have been observed and studied in science, philosophy, and religion throughout the ages. I've come to think of them as the basic facts of life – formless, foundational elements which can be observed only through their effects:

▶ There is an energy and intelligence behind life. This is ever present but is not 'in control' – it has no inherent morality or apparent point of view. It simply ensures that but for the interference of external circumstance, acorns become oak trees, cuts heal, and life begets life. (*The Principle of Mind*)

▶ The capacity to be aware and experience life is innate in human beings. It is a universal phenomenon. Our level of awareness in any given moment determines the quality of our experience. (*The Principle of Consciousness*)

▶ We create our individual experience of reality via the vehicle of thought. Thought is the missing link between the formless world of pure potentiality and the created world of form. (*The Principle of Thought*)

Let's take a deeper look at each of these principles in turn...

THE GOD PRINCIPLE: MIND

> *You know the Eastern philosophers say: 'Big Mind, little mind.' And here's the paradox: the little mind is the ego mind, that's the self-centred 'me,' the big hotshot – the only thing in the world worth looking at in the mirror is 'me.'*
>
> *The big Mind is the Divine Mind – the Universal Mind, which is the intelligence of literally all things in this world or any other world. That's the Mind you should be looking for. That's the Mind that has the power to guide you through life.*
>
> SYD BANKS

This always sounds like the set-up to a joke, even to me, but I once had a conversation about the principle of Mind with a Catholic, a Jehovah's Witness, and an atheist. They were each sharing their view of God, and not unexpectedly the conversation became somewhat heated.

The atheist turned to me and said, 'What do you think, Michael?' no doubt counting on my rational mind to come to his aid in the argument.

I reflected for a moment, and said, 'I know two things for sure: I seem to be part of a larger whole, and I'm not in charge of how things unfold. If you want to call that larger whole or great unfolding "life" or "the universe" or "spirit," I'm okay with that. If you want to call it "God," I'm okay with that too.'

To my slight surprise, all three of them were comfortable with that explanation, but as I reflected on it some more, I realized that it wasn't so surprising. After all, however we explain it, most of us realize that we're not running the show.

In mystical circles, this energy behind life is often referred to as the 'Ground of Being'; in physics, it's sometimes referred to as the 'quantum field'; in religion, it's God, or more specifically the Godhead. While to equate these things may seem heretical in some traditions (including atheism), I mean no offense by it – I'm simply pointing to the fact that nearly all traditions and fields of study point to *something* that's beyond our personal human-sized view of life.

I like to think of it as *infinite creative potential* – the potential for any form to arise (including thought-forms) and for any experience to be experienced.

In *The God Delusion*, Richard Dawkins quotes Albert Einstein:

> *'To sense that behind anything that can be experienced there is a something that our mind cannot grasp and whose beauty and sublimity reaches us only indirectly and as a feeble reflection, this is religiousness. In this sense, I am religious.'*

Dawkins then goes on to say that in this sense he too is religious. And in this sense I think anyone who has ever contemplated the miracle of life would call themselves religious, no matter what their view on a supernatural deity.

In my experience, when you begin to look beyond your personal mind to the impersonal 'big Mind,' you find something profound waiting for you there. But I was still quite coy about speaking openly about this gateway to spirit until I attended a talk given by the brilliant Principles-based psychiatrist William Pettit. He was asked about how he introduced the idea of a divine Mind to the soldiers he was treating in Iraq and other parts of the Middle East for post-traumatic stress disorder. His answer stuck with me, as I suspect it will with you:

> *'I've never met a man who's held another man's head in the scope of his rifle who hasn't already spent a great deal of time contemplating what life is and where it comes from.'*

In fact I've yet to meet anyone who hasn't at least some awareness of a part of themselves that exists beyond whatever personal trials and tribulations we all face. And the more time we spend connected with that part of ourselves, the more beautiful our life, and the impact of that life, becomes.

THE AWARENESS PRINCIPLE: CONSCIOUSNESS

> *Consciousness gives us the ability to realize the existence of life. Consciousness has an infinite number of levels; you will never come to the end of Consciousness. It is literally impossible, because Consciousness is infinite – there is no end to it. And that's a beautiful thing to know, because it means to say there is no end of you finding beauty, love and understanding in this world.*
>
> SYD BANKS

Consciousness is like a kind of developing fluid for mental photographs, bringing whatever passes through its field to life. It's the light that illuminates a film strip – the special-effects department that takes the illusion and makes it seem real. It informs our senses and brings whatever we're thinking to life.

While pure Consciousness is a formless potential, as individuals we all experience life at different levels. It's like being in a glass elevator – the world looks different depending on what floor we're on. And the elevator of our personal consciousness goes up and down all day long. When our level changes, our view changes right along with it: the higher our level, the clearer our view.

What I find so hopeful in this metaphor is that it's possible for any one of us to make a 'vertical leap' in consciousness at any time. Each new insight we have into the nature of the human condition opens up a higher perspective, a deeper understanding, and a clearer view of what's really going on. It's like making the move from an elevator that runs between the fifth and fifteenth floors of a building to one that will take us up to the twentieth floor. While we'll most assuredly continue to experience the ups and downs of life, our access to common sense, wisdom, and well-being grows exponentially with each leap.

The simplest way to gauge your current level of consciousness is to tune in to your feelings. When you're feeling low (angry, frustrated, stressed out, uncomfortable, unwell, etc.), chances are that your level of consciousness has dipped and your view of yourself, your life, and the world is relatively limited. When your mood is higher and you're feeling peaceful, loving, and content, chances are that the elevator of consciousness has begun to climb, and from these higher levels you'll naturally be able to respond more insightfully to whatever is happening around you.

Now this isn't to say that if you're feeling happy and peaceful today you're automatically in the same state of consciousness as the Buddha. But the more you look in the direction of what's *creating* experience and away from the *content* of that experience, the easier it is to hear the quiet wisdom that can lead to a quantum leap in consciousness.

THE CREATIVE PRINCIPLE: THOUGHT

Remember – and this is very important – you're only one thought away from happiness, you're only one thought away from sadness. The secret lies in Thought. It's the missing link that everybody in this world is looking for... It's a gift that we were given to have the freedom to walk through life and see what we want to see. How much better than that can you get? That you have the freedom to walk through life and see as a free thinker, that is the greatest gift ever, to be a free thinker.

SYD BANKS

When I first heard practitioners of the Three Principles talk about the principle of Thought in semi-rapturous tones, I thought that at best they were a bit simple and at worst a bit brainwashed. After all, I already knew that people thought. It hardly seemed worth mentioning, let alone waxing rhapsodic about.

But then one of my mentors pointed out the nature of what he called 'ordinary miracles' – those things that on the one hand are truly extraordinary and on the other happen so consistently that we take them completely for granted. Things like the sun appearing in the sky and not only lighting our days but also warming and nourishing life on our planet. Or gravity keeping us fixed to the Earth when every other law of physics would have us hurtling out into space.

Thought is all around us, which in some ways makes it largely invisible to us. Without thought, there would be no delineation in our world – no perception, no distinction, and no variety of experience. It's both creator and substance of our beliefs and values; it's the raw material of our hopes and dreams.

While most of us are aware of Thought at the level of what we think about life, we tend to be unaware of how much of life itself is created and maintained by Thought. Much of what appears to be solid and real is actually part of the illusion of our personal thinking.

To better understand this idea, consider an iceberg. Icebergs appear solid, but they're actually made up of the water that surrounds them. In the world of form, this means that a tiny degree of fluctuation in temperature can completely eliminate icebergs that have been in place for hundreds of years and create new ones seemingly out of nowhere. In the inner world of the formless, it means that no matter how solid the foundations of your reality may seem, it only takes a slight shift in consciousness for your entire world to change.

To me, this is one of the most exciting things about Thought. It's at the heart of everything we experience, from monsters to angels and from problems to possibilities. And since we have an infinite potential for new thought, we're only ever one new thought away from a completely different experience of being alive.

PUTTING IT ALL TOGETHER

I'll let Syd Banks finish this section with a summary of how these principles fit together:

What are Mind, Consciousness, and Thought?

Mind is the intelligence of all things; Consciousness makes you aware; and Thought is like the rudder of a ship. It guides you through life, and if you learn to use that rudder properly, you can guide your way through life far better than you ever imagined. You can go from one reality to another. You can find your happiness and when illusionary sadness comes from memories, you don't try to figure it out. Please don't try to do that – you'll get yourself in trouble. All you have to do is realize that it's Thought.

The second you realize that it's Thought, you are touching the very essence of psychological experience. You're back to the 'now,' you're back to happiness. So don't get caught up on a lot of details...

When you're ready, you will find what you're looking for. I don't care who you are. I don't care where you are. If you're in the middle of the Sahara Desert ... and it's time for you to find the answer, the right person will appear in the middle of the desert and let you know. He will say something to you that will trigger something inside you.

And that's where that life comes from: inside out. It's spiritual knowledge. It's there, everybody has it and people don't realize that. There's no human being more spiritual than you – everybody is equal.

And you know what the equality is?

That we all derive from Mind, Consciousness, and Thought.

That's the equalizer. And while you have that equalizer you're as good as anybody on this Earth, you're as holy as anybody else on this Earth. You always have been, always will be; the only thing is you don't see it because of your thoughts.

In the next chapter we'll take a look at the revolutionary implications of these three principles for the way we experience our lives. But first, here are a few thoughts to reflect on:

▶ A principle is something that's fundamental – true for all people at all times, with no exceptions.

▶ Our experience of life can be understood via three fundamental principles: Mind, Consciousness, and Thought.

▶ To put it another way, everything we experience in life is a function of three spiritual facts: we are alive, we are aware, and we think.

▶ We're only ever one new thought away from a completely different experience of being alive.

THE ONLY THING YOU NEED TO KNOW

*'A man will be imprisoned in a room
with a door that's unlocked and opens
inwards as long as it does not occur
to him to pull rather than push.'*

Ludwig Wittgenstein

When I first began sharing the Three Principles with my clients, I noticed that we would reach a certain breakthrough point in our work together after which nothing was ever the same again. The clients may have been successful and even relatively happy before that point, but after it, the very basis of their lives somehow shifted.

Clients described their experience of this transformative moment in a variety of ways, from 'So that's what you've been talking about all this time' to 'Nothing's changed, but everything's different' to 'The butterfly has landed.'

What I wasn't clear about for awhile was what exactly had happened at that point. I was certainly aware that they'd all had a deeper insight into something; I just wasn't sure what that something was.

When I began asking other Principles-based practitioners if they saw the same 'breakthrough insight' in their work, they universally knew what I was talking about. The consensus was that the real 'game changer' with people was the moment they had a deeper insight into the inside-out nature of reality.

The prevailing model in our culture is that our experience of life is created from the outside in – that is, what happens to us on the outside determines our experience on the inside. People or circumstances 'make' us happy, angry, sad, fearful, or loving, and the game of life is to find, attract, create, or manifest the right people and circumstances in order to have more of the good feelings and fewer of the bad ones.

One variation on this model (which I call 'empowered outside in') argues that it's not so much what happens to us as what we do with what happens to us that determines our experience. If we rise to the challenge, we can go from reacting as victims of the events of life to responding as creators, making lemonade out of lemons and creating the relationships and circumstances that will bring us happiness and fulfillment.

A second variation (which I call 'enlightened outside in') says that while people and circumstances certainly matter, what's even more important is what we think about those people and circumstances. Everything from Cognitive and Rational-Emotive therapy to the majority of the self-help movement points out that if you can replace a negative thought, belief, or attitude toward people and circumstances with a positive one, not only will your experience change immediately, but before long the people and circumstances will likely change as well – and even if they don't, at least your positive thoughts and attitudes will allow you to make the best of a bad situation.

While both of these variations certainly promote greater effectiveness in the workplace and a more enjoyable experience of being alive, they're limited in the scope of their impact not by the lack of discipline or skill of the practitioners, but rather because they're rooted in a fundamentally inaccurate model.

By way of explanation, imagine the following scenario:

You're in an art studio filled with painters standing at their easels. Although you can't see it from where you're standing, they're all looking in the direction of a small platform in the center of the room and painting what they see.

As you walk around the studio, you notice small and sometimes vast discrepancies between what people are painting on their canvases. Arguments break out in parts of the room as to whether or not the model for the painting is more one color than another, taller or shorter, uglier or more beautiful than rendered.

You begin to become curious about what it is that everyone's painting, so you make your way to the center of the room and discover to your surprise that there's absolutely nothing there. The emptiness of the center is palpable.

Suddenly, you realize the reason why everyone's painting a different picture isn't down to their point of view, where their easel happens to be placed, or even to a matter of personal interpretation. It's because what they are 'viewing' is only a projection of their own thoughts.

The moment you catch even a glimpse of the illusory nature of the world of form, the game of life changes completely and irrevocably. No matter how scary or oppressive or insecure your experience of life may be, once you realize that it's only your own thinking that you're experiencing, that thinking loses much of its hold over you. You may still feel uncomfortable feelings, but because you know that what's causing them isn't *outside* you, you don't feel compelled to change the world in order to change the way you feel, any more than you would go to your television set to try to convince the characters on your favorite soap opera to change their foolish ways.

What Syd Banks saw when he had his enlightenment experience was that we live in a world of thought. Not a world influenced by thought, where positive outperforms negative and gives us a 'competitive advantage in the marketplace,' but *a world that is actually created from thought*. And the moment we stop fighting with ourselves and others about *what* to think and instead focus on the miracle that we *are* thinking, the details of life begin to work themselves out, all by themselves.

The simple truth is this:

Our experience of life is created from the inside out via the principles of Mind, Consciousness, and Thought. We're living in the feeling of our thinking, not the feeling of the world.

We're simply not designed to experience an outside world in any other way. We can't see, hear, or feel without thought informing our senses, and we have no way of checking whether or not our thoughts are telling us about something that's really happening or simply projecting false data which we then interpret as true. That's why one moment we can be sure that everything's going to be fine and the next we can be equally sure that it isn't – without anything actually changing in the world.

This inability to verify our observations doesn't mean that the world doesn't exist – just that its impact on our experience of life has been vastly exaggerated.

HOW REAL IS OUR REALITY?

To better understand the inside-out paradigm, let's step into the glass elevator of consciousness and see how the world changes when viewed from different levels of understanding.

Ground Floor: Objective Reality

> *'What I see is what's really happening.*
> *I'm experiencing the world as it is.'*

At the bottom of the elevator, the world of form looks 100 per cent real to us. We think of the mind as being like a camera which is accurately recording what's going on outside us, and everything it tells us about that objective reality is taken as the absolute truth: our boss really is a jerk, we truly are being taken advantage of, and life actually *is* easier for everyone else than it is for us. If we want to change our experience, the only way to do it is to change the world.

While we all have certain perceptions that we're convinced are completely and objectively true, people who get stuck down in the basement of consciousness often end up on the streets, in mental institutions, or in prisons. This happens in all innocence, as it's understandably difficult to function in society when you can't tell the difference between a thought and reality.

Lower Floors: Subjective Reality

'What I see is an interpretation of reality. I'm experiencing the world through the filter of my thinking.'

As our level of understanding increases and the elevator rises, we begin to experience a slight separation between our personal thinking and the idea of an objective reality. While the mind still appears to function as a camera, we can see that how we frame the picture and what filter or lens we look through will affect the way things appear to us. This is the world of subjective reality, and it's the level at which many psychologies and self-help philosophies suggest we make our stand.

At this level of understanding, it seems that what happens in the world influences us, but its impact can be mitigated by changing or controlling our thoughts. So, if we want to feel better, we try to change our beliefs, reframe our circumstances, and become more mindful in ways that lessen the impact of stressful, frightening, or otherwise difficult situations and heighten the impact of positive ones.

The reason this is still a variant on the outside-in model is that stress, fear, and difficulty are perceived to be primary characteristics of the *situation*, not of our own thinking. And here we can draw a simple line in the sand:

Any time an internal experience is considered to be an inherent property of something other than Mind, Consciousness, and Thought in the moment, we're living in an outside-in interpretation of the world.

Higher Floors: Constructed Reality

'What I see is all made up.
The world is what I think it is.'

As we deepen our understanding and move up in consciousness, we begin to see that the nature of thought is both creative and arbitrary. Instead of trying to explain why we think what we think by looking for evidence in the world or in our upbringing, we recognize the mind is not so much a camera as a paintbrush and, consciously or unconsciously, we are the artist.

At this level of understanding, we recognize that:

▶ We don't experience money; we experience our thinking about money.

▶ We don't experience our children, parents, or partners; we experience our thinking about our children, parents, and partners.

▶ We don't experience the world; we experience our thinking about the world.

This level of understanding opens up the possibility of making dramatic changes in our lives and transforming our relationships with others. We become less inclined to over-react to the whirlwind of our ever-changing thoughts and more able to respond insightfully to both gradual and sudden shifts in our circumstances.

Top Floors: Illusory Reality

'There is no separation between "out there" and "in here." But for my thinking, I am a pure expression of the energy of life.'

At the level of illusion, the mind is seen to work less as a camera or paintbrush than as a kaleidoscope, creating endless patterns of experience as it diffracts the oneness of life via the prism of Thought. This is the level of understanding that invites the miraculous – transformations that defy rational explanation and insights that redefine the world in which we live.

While mystics throughout the ages seem to agree that the formless world of spirit is reality and the world of form is just illusion, any Zen master worth their salt will hit you over the head with a stick or drop a large rock on your foot the second you start claiming that you 'really do know that it's all just thought.' But for those of us lucky enough to catch a glimpse of the illusory nature of reality, even for a moment, the world changes. 'Reality' becomes a little bit more fluid, and we begin to experience a level of calm and peace that may have previously been unimaginable to us. In those moments of clear seeing, lives change.

While I certainly don't live at this level of consciousness, even knowing it exists is often enough to give me hope when I bump up against something that seems so solid and hurts so much that I hear myself saying, 'Sure, I get that all that other stuff was just thought, but *this* isn't my thinking – this is *real*!'

How we deal with those moments will be a later topic in our conversation. For now, here's a real-life example of how quickly a deeper understanding of the inside-out nature of reality can lead to change.

ALICE IN CHAINS

Alice was the wife of a client I'd been seeing for only a short time when she requested a session with me. When we sat down together, she told me almost immediately that she was fed up and wanted to leave my client and take the kids with her.

She burst into tears and vented her frustration at his mercurial mood swings, neuroses, and inability to follow through on his promises. The last straw was a proposed trip to the Caribbean which had been canceled at the last minute when he'd panicked about everything from missing out on potential work to the plane crashing if the rest of the family went on without him.

As much as I liked my client, it really seemed to me that his wife had a point. But I knew enough to just keep listening. After a time, Alice's litany of complaints drew to a close and she finished by saying, 'It feels mean-spirited of me because I know he's going through a tough time, but I don't know how anyone could live with this level of frustration!'

I asked her if she was open to some coaching, and when she said yes, I shared a little about how reality is created from the inside out. We talked about how frustration isn't feedback about our life but feedback about the quality of our thinking at a particular moment. In a clearer state of mind, thoughts of frustration might still arise, but we won't give them a second thought. When our mind is relatively clear, our personal thinking just doesn't get traction in the same way that it does when our head is cluttered.

So, while I couldn't advise her on what to do, one thing I could say with absolute certainty was that she wasn't in a fit state to make a good decision about what to have for lunch, let alone about whether or not she should be leaving her husband.

After a few moments of quiet, she looked at me and her eyes lit up for the first time since we'd started talking.

'I don't want to leave him,' she said. 'I love him – I really, really do. It's just been hard seeing him go through this and it makes me feel like a failure as a wife because I can't make everything okay.'

We spoke for another 20 minutes or so and she thanked me and that was that.

I only heard from her directly once after that, about six weeks later via an e-mail. She thanked me for our conversation and said that things had been much, much better since we'd spoken.

'I don't always see it in the moment,' she wrote, 'but just knowing that I'm feeling my thinking and not my life makes all the difference in the world.'

About a year later, I got a postcard from my client – he was on holiday with his family and everything was going extremely well.

What struck me was how quickly Alice got something that had taken me nearly 40 years of my life to see.

This was by no means the first time I'd seen someone's world shift in a single session. When it first started happening, I went to my coach at the time, Sandy Krot, and asked her if she could explain how problems that seemed ingrained and intractable could resolve themselves in a matter of minutes. She simply said, 'Because they were never really there in the first place.'

She went on to share a story about a client of George Pransky's who got upset with him for implying that his problems weren't real.

'Are you trying to tell me,' the client said, 'that none of what I'm feeling is real?'

'The *feelings* are real,' George responded, 'but the way you're seeing your life isn't. It's just a trick of the mind, like a mirage.'

'So you're saying,' the client continued, 'that I'm feeling all of this stress and pressure because of a mirage?'

George reflected for a moment.

'Well,' he replied, 'it's a real mirage.'

PUTTING IT ALL TOGETHER

As we continue along in our conversation together, some of the ideas we talk about may challenge your views of what's real and what's possible. I ask only for you to stay open to the possibility that even the most solid looking and seemingly unchangeable problems in your life might, when viewed from higher up the elevator of consciousness, appear as curious to you as a person painting a picture of a monster and then running out of the room screaming in terror.

Syd Banks used to say:

> 'The world is a divine dream, suspended between
> the boundaries of time, space, and matter.'

And while we may never wake up from the dream, it's possible at any moment to wake up to the fact that we're dreaming.

In the next part of our conversation, we'll look more deeply into the nature of the inside-out understanding and how it can lead us toward seemingly miraculous transformations, life-changing insights, and a calmer, wiser experience of life.

Before we move on, here are some thoughts to reflect on:

▶ People think experience is coming at them from the outside in, but it's actually coming through them from the inside out.

▶ We're living in the feeling of our thinking, not the feeling of the world.

▶ 'Reality' changes when viewed from different levels of understanding.

▶ The more we understand where our experience is coming from, the less frightened we'll be of that experience.

▶ When our thoughts look real, we live in a world of suffering. When they look subjective, we live in a world of choice. When they look arbitrary, we live in a world of possibility. And when we see them as illusory, we wake up inside a world of dreams.

2

EXPANDING POSSIBILITIES

'Most people live, whether physically, intellectually, or morally, in a very restricted circle of their potential being.'

William James

A FORMULA
FOR MIRACLES

'You do not need to leave your room.
Remain sitting at your table and listen.
Do not even listen, simply wait.
Do not even wait, be quite still and solitary.
The world will freely offer itself to you
to be unmasked. It has no choice.
It will roll in ecstasy at your feet.'

Franz Kafka

I first came across the field of coaching in 1988 when a friend plunked me in front of a set of Tony Robbins audio cassettes and asked me to listen with her. A few hundred hours of reading, listening, and live training later, I launched my first coaching company with my best friend David. We called it Momentum, because at the time it seemed to us that the secret of success was Newton's First Law of Motion:

An object at rest tends to stay at rest; an object in motion tends to stay in motion.

We figured that the most helpful thing we could do with our students and clients was to assist them in jump-starting their projects, careers, and lives, and getting up such a head of steam that it would be almost easier to keep going than to stop. However, while this approach certainly made a difference for a number of people, it was also apparent that going faster didn't really help when you were headed in the wrong direction.

So, a few years later, having studied the work of Steven R. Covey and Dr. Richard Bandler, I decided that the 'real' secret of success was to change our thoughts and actions so that we did less of what didn't work and more of what did. I called my new company Behavior Changes, and I began to work with companies, groups, and individuals on a largely behavioral level, seeking to eliminate their 'bad' or unproductive habits while simultaneously installing 'good' productive ones.

For the next decade or so, I enjoyed working with people to change their programmed habits of thinking and behavior, sometimes directly, sometimes through the development of skills, and often through an exploration of their most deeply held beliefs and values. I became one of the top coaches and trainers in my field, but it troubled me that the clients who seemed to experience the biggest positive shifts weren't necessarily the ones who achieved their stated goals for our work together.

Whether my clients were trying to change their lives by changing the world, changing their actions, or changing their thoughts, they were still laboring under a fundamentally false assumption: the idea that if they could somehow gain control over their circumstances (including the 'circumstances' of their thoughts), their experience of life would change for the better.

While each of these three types of intervention can provide short-term relief when successful, over time they often create as many problems as they solve. We become wealthier, more successful, and find somebody to love, only to now fill our time protecting our wealth, hanging on to our success, and worrying about losing the one we love.

Or we become more disciplined, change our habits, and get ourselves on track, but always know that we're only a few bad days or weeks away from backsliding further than we've worked so hard to come.

Or we affirm abundance and health, eliminate the luxury of a negative thought, only hang out with 'positive people,' and wonder why our world has become so small and tight and restricted.

So, if chasing better results, changing our behavior, and controlling our thoughts won't get us what we really want, what will? How do we find the difference that makes the difference?

TRANSFORMATION FOR DUMMIES

There's a famous cartoon by Sidney Harris featuring two men at a chalk board:

"I THINK YOU SHOULD BE MORE EXPLICIT HERE IN STEP TWO."

While the cartoon is clearly poking more fun at mathematics than psychology, the same three-step formula often seems to apply whenever people undergo a transformative shift in their life:

❯ *Step One:* They live their life, doing the best they can but often drifting or even floundering along the way.

❯ *Step Two:* Then a miracle occurs...

❯ *Step Three:* ...and somehow their life is completely different. They go from inaction to action, from stuck to flowing, from limited to free, from miserable to happy. They're no longer driven to drink alcohol or go shopping or take regular hits of their drug of choice. Before long, their career takes off, their relationships improve beyond all recognition, and their creative output soars.

We all know at least one person who's experienced this kind of transformation in their life. Perhaps it's a friend or family member who 'found religion' and really did begin to live a kinder, gentler life. Or someone who was diagnosed with a life-threatening illness or had a near-death experience and began to experience more gratitude and to appreciate the simple things in life.

Sometimes, the cause of the transformation seems more random – the person read something in a book, or heard someone say something that somehow struck them at a far deeper level than may have been intended.

Syd Banks reportedly experienced his first major insight while hiking with a fellow participant on a weekend seminar. In the midst of an argument over which of them was more insecure, his companion told him, 'You're not *really* insecure, Syd – you just think you are.' Somehow, that innocuous, almost comical statement made nearly 40 years ago triggered a series of insights into the nature of Mind, Thought, and Consciousness which led to the development of a whole new field of psychology.

Such transformations are not the result of an intervention, but rather the effect of a shift in our level of consciousness.

Most of us experienced at least a temporary shift in our level of consciousness the first time we fell in love. Suddenly, the world seemed a more beautiful place. We were inspired to write poetry, or to draw pictures, or create things that reflected the beautiful feelings we felt inside us.

Because we attributed those feelings to another person, we often returned to our habitual level afterward. But those feelings don't come from outside us – they're a part of our essential selves. When we see the fundamental truth of that, the shift in consciousness becomes permanent and new levels of seeing become available to us. That transformative shift comes to us via insight – literally 'sight from within.'

Insights are those wonderful 'Aha!' moments when we're able to see something about ourselves, our life, or life itself in a whole new way. People often call them 'light-bulb moments,' because we see things in a new light that makes them look less fixed and less scary than before. If there's anything to be done, we do it without the need for any additional debate or willpower.

In these wonderful transformative moments, we discover a fresh new way of seeing something that we may have been looking at for ages. We suddenly 'get it' – not intellectually, the way we might understand a concept, but at an almost cellular level, the way we either get a joke or we don't, even when we know that it's supposed to be funny. Quite simply, insights change our world.

THE INSIGHT FAIRY

Unfortunately, knowing that we need to have insights in order to transform used to feel a bit discouraging to me. While I'd certainly had wonderful insights throughout my life, short of trying to force a breakthrough or praying to the 'insight fairy' (which oddly seemed to work a little bit better than trying to force a breakthrough, despite the fact that I'm fairly sure there is no 'insight fairy'), I always felt that getting a great insight more than once or twice a year was too much to hope for.

Which is why I was so delighted when I had my first real insight into insights:

All an 'insight' really is... is a new thought.

For me, that realization was a game changer because I knew I could have fresh thinking at any moment. It's not a big deal or a mystical process – it's just a part of the nature of Thought. Our thinking changes moment by moment, so the ability to have a new thought about an old situation is natural and ever present.

The most impactful of these 'new thoughts' seem to arise from somewhere beyond our personal databank, and contain information and wisdom outside our current knowledge. They're a part of the natural intelligence of Mind, and we experience them as common sense and innate wisdom.

This now allows us to write up our 'formula for miracles' in the form of two simple psycho-spiritual equations:

Mind + Thought + Consciousness = Reality

Mind + New Thought + Consciousness = New Reality

And it also allows us to be 'more explicit in step two.' If we replace '*Then a miracle occurs…*' with '*Then a new thought comes to mind*,' we have a formula that's considerably more reliable, practical, and predictive:

▶ *Step One:* We look in the direction of what's true in life, as opposed to searching for the most useful lie.

▶ *Step Two:* As we see more truth, we experience more new thinking and a river of insights begins to flow.

❱ *Step Three:* When an insight is sufficiently profound, its impact on our life is transformative. Nothing changes on the outside, but everything's different on the inside. We experience a vertical leap in our level of consciousness and gain new perspective on our old way of being in the world.

For those of us interested in well-being (or indeed the well-being of the planet), this formula for miracles takes us to a fork in the road. We can continue down the path of control and attempt to think, behave, or change the world in our quest for happiness and well-being. In fairness, this path has numerous advantages. It's well lit and well traveled and we'll rarely find ourselves at a loss for companions on that journey. While these companions may disagree with us on the specific things we need to change or how to change them, they'll never question the fundamental premise that we need to change something in order to be happy and whole.

On the other hand, we can take the path of transformation, sacrificing that comforting feeling of being in control in the hope of discovering greater freedom. We give up on the apparent safety of the known in search of the as yet unknown – the field of pure possibility – the space where miracles happen.

I sometimes compare the contrast between the path of control and the path of transformation as the difference between climbing a ladder and taking the elevator. When we see our own actions, thoughts, and intentions as the primary motive force in creating change, we do our best to soldier on up the infinite ladder of consciousness, climbing ten rungs today and slipping back down eight tomorrow.

But when we see that consciousness itself is the greatest transformative force available, we simply step into the elevator of insight, hanging out in the unknown and looking into the mystery of being alive. While we don't control the timing, each time the doors of perception open we emerge from the elevator on a higher floor, with a new, clearer view of life.

Of course, at times the elevator may go down as well as up. But once we've had an insight and seen the view from a higher floor, we can never really forget it.

PUTTING IT ALL TOGETHER

In the next chapter, we'll take a closer look at the deeper intelligence of Mind and the kindness of the design. Before we do, here are a few of the main ideas from this chapter:

‣ Interventions tend to address symptoms without fundamentally correcting the source of our problems – a misunderstanding of where our experience is coming from.

‣ An insight is a new thought, containing information and wisdom outside our current knowledge.

▶ Insights change our world.

▶ Mind + New Thought + Consciousness = New Reality

▶ When we give up on trying to control our experience, we find ourselves moving effortlessly into higher levels of consciousness.

5

ORIGINAL GRACE

'I am the happiest man alive.
I have that in me that can convert
poverty to riches, adversity to prosperity.
I am more invulnerable than Achilles;
fortune hath not one place to hit me.'

Sir Thomas Brown

My own first major insight into the inside-out nature of reality came when I traveled to that small town near the Canadian border and had my first four-day conversation with Dr. Keith Blevens, a member of George Pransky's team. I was convinced that I was going to learn their secret techniques for dissolving problems and take them home so that I could incorporate them into my work. But two days into our time together, I realized that all we'd talked about was the nature of Mind, Consciousness, and Thought, and how they combined to create our experience of life. Pleasant though the conversation was, I was waiting with increasing impatience for him to get to the point.

By the second night, when I popped a recording of Syd Banks talking about the power of Thought into the DVD player in my hotel room, I'd just about given up on learning anything of value. Then, halfway through my second beer, I heard something so profound that the beer came spurting out my nose as I burst into fits of laughter.

All Syd said (and I've gone back and played the DVD over again to check) was:

'Every human being has innate mental health.'

The reason it struck me as funny was because somehow I knew that it was absolutely and fundamentally true.

I had been a depressed, suicidal teen. And as I learned and practiced many of the self-help techniques that proliferate in our culture, it got better. For over 15 years I studied and practiced every methodology I could find to stave off depression and 'create' positive feelings in my body. And I became convinced that the only things preventing me from sliding back into the misery I had fought tooth and nail to escape were my techniques and practices. So for Syd to say that mental health was natural went against everything I'd learned – and taught – in my first forays into the world of self-help.

Yet I could instantly see the truth of it. After all, babies don't need therapy. And while I can't honestly say I remember what it felt like to be in the womb, I knew from watching my own kids grow up that, other than during periods of physical discomfort, they lived in a pretty continual state of mental well-being for the first few years of their lives. In seeing the original grace of my innate mental health, I felt as though the burden of nearly 40 years of struggle had been lifted off my shoulders.

Well-being is our nature. That doesn't mean we always feel good – any one of us can get caught up in thought at any time, and in so doing become instantly subject to every emotional color in the spectrum. But to say that means that well-being comes and goes would be like saying that because there are clouds, the sun isn't always present. Even in the darkest hour, the sun is still there – it's just that sometimes there's something between us and our clear seeing.

ON HAVING A NOSE

Shortly after I had this insight, a potential client named Richard came to my office and asked me if I could help him.

'I see people all around me who are happy and it seems so unfair,' he began. 'I'm not a bad person. I always try to do my best. Don't I deserve a bit of happiness in my life too?'

To my dismay, I felt myself starting to crack up. I tried to stifle the laughter because I knew it was horribly inappropriate, but I wound up snorting instead. Richard briefly took offense, but I caught my breath, regained my bearings, and, as gently as I could, pointed out the essential humor in his request. It was as though someone had come to me saying, 'Can you help me? I see people all around me with noses and it seems so unfair. I'm not a bad person. Don't I deserve to have a nose on my face too?'

As we spoke further, Richard and I explored some of the other things he thought he needed to practice in order to have.

'I'd like to open my heart more,' he said. 'Is there something I could do to get better at opening my heart?'

At that moment, my then five-year-old daughter Maisy ran into my office, asking whether she could go outside to catch some fairies.

I said yes (after all, I'm not an ogre), and then returned to my conversation with Richard.

'Do you think Maisy needs to practice keeping her heart open?' I asked him.

'Well, no, but she's just a child. She hasn't learned to close her heart yet.'

We left those words sitting in the silence for some moments, which I finally broke with this quote from Arnold Patent in his book *Money*:

'We don't create abundance.
Abundance is always present.
We create limitation.'

We don't need to create abundance, because abundance is already there. We don't need to create love, or well-being, or happiness, because love, well-being, and happiness are part of our essential nature. We don't need to learn to open our heart or connect with others, because that's just what happens when we don't stop it from happening.

Do you need to practice not stepping on the accelerator of your car if you'd like to slow down? Not really – because as soon as you notice that you're the one stepping on the accelerator, you can stop any time you like.

Similarly, the moment you actually notice you're closing down your heart or cutting off your good feelings for another person (because, after all, they left their socks on the floor, or didn't say 'thank you,' or ran into your office when you were with a client), you'll probably just stop, because you have an innate common sense that tells you that if you keep shooting yourself in the foot, you might want to put down the gun before you go in for toe surgery.

The return to this 'original grace' of life is always available to us, and takes no particular effort to attain because it is in fact a return to our natural way of being. Here's all you need to know:

There's nothing you need to do, be, have, get, change, practice, or learn in order to be happy, loving, and whole.

RESTORING THE FACTORY DEFAULTS

Our innate well-being is just one of what I've come to recognize as the 'factory default settings' for human beings. I first came up with this analogy after struggling to get my computer printer working for nearly a week and finally deciding I needed professional help. Given that I'd tried everything I could think of and every little tweak and addition to the system that the online forums had to offer, I was a bit disappointed when the professional's help was so simple – he told me to click the button marked 'Restore to default.' Sure enough, after a couple of minutes of clicking and whirring, my printer was back online and I was left reflecting on what the equivalent of clicking that button would be for us human beings.

The more I reflected, the more apparent it became to me that so many of the things we strive to achieve in our personal development are actually a part of our 'factory settings.' For example, perhaps the most beautiful feeling available to us is the deep connection we can experience with another human being, a beloved pet, or even the world around us. So this would certainly seem to be worth striving and maybe even struggling to achieve, a fact to which the millions of people who continue to search for true love in spite of the seemingly overwhelming odds of finding it bear witness. But once again, we have it backward.

In order to want to feel more connected, we first have to separate ourselves out. As anyone with young children knows, this game of individuation starts early, as the borders of the body start to feel more solid and the words 'I,' 'me,' and 'mine' start to take on more and more meaning and importance.

Then, as we get older, we put up more boundaries between ourselves and the whole, defining ourselves as separate not just in terms of our body but also our religion, our ethnicity, our beliefs, and our values. This active separation is what makes connectedness seem such a worthy goal.

But the truth is we're already connected to life, because we're made of the same energy as all living things. Like waves in a cosmic ocean, we appear to be separate without ever separating from the whole.

Or consider how much time is spent in personal and spiritual development seminars on 'being present.' I have a completely untested theory that every ten years or so someone comes along saying 'The present moment is a good thing' in just the right way for society to go: 'Holy cow, this is brilliantly insightful – when we're not up in our heads all the time, we're more powerful and enjoy our lives more!'

So we all strive for more now-ness in our life, using whichever meditation or mindfulness practice is in vogue in our particular world. Yet 'being here now' is the default: we have to think our way out of the present moment, and the moment we stop doing it, we're right back where we started – right where we are sitting now.

THE INTELLIGENCE BEHIND THE SYSTEM

A couple of years ago, Nina and I spent our second honeymoon on the islands of Bora Bora. One day, a South African expat was complaining to us that it was difficult to get good help on his vanilla plantation, as the locals had ready access to everything they needed there on the island with no need for money to go out and buy it.

In the same way, as we see that so much of what we're striving for is there for the taking, it makes less and less sense to work so hard for what we already have. When you don't drink rat poison, you don't need an antidote. And when separating yourself out from the whole, planning and remembering your way out of the present moment, and thinking your way out of well-being stop seeming like good ideas, you do them less and less. At some point, the system resets, and you get a fresh start.

To better understand how your experience of life can change for the better without you having to do the changing, imagine waking up from a nightmare. One moment you're totally engrossed in fighting off vampire zombies and the next your eyes are open and the vampire zombies are gone. You may still have a little bit of adrenaline coursing through your veins, but there are no lasting after-effects. No healing is necessary. You just get up and get on with your day.

In the same way, no healing is necessary after an unpleasant or insecure thought – you just wake up (to the fact of your thinking) and before long a new thought comes along and you have a new experience. While the new thought isn't necessarily better than the old one, when we just allow thoughts to pass through us, the intelligence behind the system seems to move in the direction of deeper thoughts and greater mental health.

This pre-existing intelligence shows up in nearly every area of life. For example, my family and I recently visited Sequoia National Park in California and went to an exhibition on forest fires. It turns out that in the early part of the twentieth century, technology and resources had gotten to the point where the number of forest fires in America's national parks dropped to an all-time low. But, to the surprise of most of the people involved in this fire prevention and suppression effort, their 'success' at controlling wildfires actually led to a less healthy eco-system.

While most of us think of forest fires as a bad thing, they're a part of the pre-existing intelligence of nature – one of the ways in which old growth is cleared away to make room for something new. Modern prevention takes this into account and allows for many naturally occurring wildland fires to run their course. They're closely monitored to prevent them from spreading into populated areas, but are allowed to play out their role in the renewal of the forest.

Another example of this pre-existing intelligence is the human body. It's designed to heal itself. If I cut my finger, I don't need to get overly involved in the process of clotting the blood, creating the scab, or growing new skin. That's the intelligence behind the physical system at work. While we think of fevers and diarrhea and vomiting as bad things, they're the body's way of eliminating toxins in a hurry. It's all built in to the design.

As far as I can tell, the same thing is true of the mind. It's designed to clear itself out all the time and to return to quiet and clarity. It's like a self-cleaning cat litter tray – the cat poops, the tray senses the extra weight, and the arm comes up and clears the poop away.

Now the moment you understand that, you're off the hook. Because the system is designed to take care of your mental hygiene, you don't have to. It's sometimes hard to trust the self-regulating nature of the system to clean out our old crappy thinking and replace it with new thought, but the intelligence behind the system is always at work – and it works the same for everyone.

We feel our thinking, and it shapes our perceptions and

creates our experience of life. This is true regardless of where we're from or how worthy we think we are. Delivering fresh thinking is just a natural part of how the system works. When we trust the process and allow it to do its job, our life becomes simpler and our experience becomes richer.

THE KINDNESS OF THE DESIGN

I heard a lovely illustration of this idea from Robert Kausen, a teacher and consultant in this approach for many years. He was telling me about a friend of his from high school who was training for his pilot's license.

During his first solo flight, he lost control of his Piper Cub 'trainer plane' high above the ground. The more he tried to bring the plane back under his control, the more wildly it span. His conversation with the tower went something like this:

Pilot: *Mayday! Mayday! I've lost control of the plane – please advise!*

Tower: *Take your hands and feet off the controls. I repeat, take your hands and feet off the controls!*

Pilot: *Negative, tower – repeat, I have lost control of the plane! I'm trying everything I can to bring it back under control, but I just can't do it! This is a matter of life and death – please, just tell me what to do!*

Tower: *This is a matter of life and death – take your hands and feet off the controls! Do it now!*

What the young pilot didn't know (and the air traffic controller clearly did) was that trainer planes have a self-righting mechanism built into them. When the pilot lets go of the controls, the plane levels itself out. Once the plane is back on an even keel, the pilot can take over again and steer the plane back to safety – which is exactly what happened in the case of Robert's young friend.

So how does this apply to us?

The principle of Mind seems to work through us in the direction of health and well-being. It's a sort of spiritual immune system that will bring a return to peace the moment we step out of the way. I wouldn't even think of trying to heal my own cut finger; I needn't try so hard to heal my wounded psyche.

The reason so few of us get to experience that power working in our life is that we're so busy trying to fix everything for ourselves. And ironically, like the pilot overworking the controls of a plane designed to right itself, our constant affirmations and interventions often get in the way of our mind's return to clarity and health.

We try so hard to remember to live by the wisdom and insights of others that we forget the source of that wisdom is inside us as well. Insights are the natural side-effects of living with a relatively quiet mind and a relatively beautiful feeling. Forget the words, stay with the feeling, and the insights will continue to unfold.

I know it can be difficult trying not to fix things when you're convinced that they're broken, and even more difficult when you're convinced that they're getting worse. But in a quieter moment (and we all have our quieter moments), consider the possibility that healthy psychological functioning is the default and your natural state is peace. And if you're willing to take your hands and feet off the controls, you just might find yourself returning to this natural state more and more and more of the time.

When you do, you'll know beyond a shadow of a doubt that that place of peace is your psychological and spiritual home.

PUTTING IT ALL TOGETHER

In the next chapter, we'll take a closer look at that place of peace – the meditative state. Until then, here are a few reminders of some of the key ideas in this chapter:

▶ Every one of us has innate mental health.

▶ There's nothing we need to do, be, have, get, change, practice, or learn in order to be happy, loving, and whole.

▶ Connection, presence, and well-being are a part of our 'factory settings.'

▶ The equivalent of our reset button is a deeper insight into the nature of the human experience.

▶ There is an intelligence behind the system and a kindness to the design.

▶ When we let go of trying to control our thoughts, this pre-existing intelligence will lead us back toward our innate wisdom and well-being.

THE VALUE OF
AN EMPTY MIND

'Leave thinking to the one who gave intelligence. In Silence there is eloquence. Stop weaving, and watch how the pattern improves.'

Rumi

For several years early on in my teaching career, I told a version of the following story at the beginning of my trainings...

> *Once upon a time, a student traveled far and wide in order to expand his knowledge of the path. Much to his delight, one day he was granted an audience with a noted Zen master. When they sat down together, he shared the many things he'd been studying on his journey.*
>
> *After listening politely for nearly an hour, the master called for tea. As always, the tea was prepared*

according to an elaborate set of rituals. When it came time to pour, the master himself performed the honors.

However, to the student's dismay, the master didn't stop pouring when the teacup was full. He continued to pour the golden liquid until it began spilling over the sides of the cup and onto the saucer. The student didn't want to be so presumptuous as to correct the master, but when the tea began to pour over the edges of the saucer and puddle on the floor, he felt he had no choice.

'Excuse me, oh venerable one,' he said, careful to observe the forms of respect, 'but you must stop pouring. The cup is full – it can take on no more tea.'

'Ah,' said the master with a twinkle in his eye. 'Like this cup, your mind is full of your own ideas and accumulated learning. If you want to learn something new, first you must empty your cup!'

I used the story as a way of encouraging people to put their old thinking to one side and 'get stupid' so that they could approach learning new things with a 'beginner's mind.' But it was only when I began studying the inside-out understanding that I caught a glimpse into a far more powerful meaning to the story. Rather than trying to make room for a new philosophy to be poured in by an 'expert' in this field or that, the point of emptying our mind is so that it can be filled with insight from the natural intelligence that exists beyond our personal thinking.

While I intuitively recognized the value of 'getting stupid,' I was also fiercely resistant to it. My mother has a Ph.D. in organic chemistry from the University of Brussels, my brother started MIT at 16, and my sister started Harvard at 17. Our family valued intellect, and I was damned if I was going to put that to one side. *After all*, I reasoned to myself, *my intellect is what's gotten me where I am today.*

So, when I hired a Principles-based practitioner named Kristen Mansheim to assist me in integrating this understanding into my work, I spent way too much time trying to persuade her of the value of intellect in general and of my intellect in particular.

What lost me the argument wasn't anything she said, but rather something I felt: in the midst of my repeated intellectual thrusts into her annoyingly non-judgmental listening, I was suddenly overwhelmed by a deep and profound feeling of peace and quiet.

In the lingering silence, I saw two things quite clearly. The first was that this sense of peace was something I recognized as having been present in several of my most life-changing moments. The second was that even if I'd never experienced it before, I would gladly have traded a thousand intellectual victories for even five extra minutes spent resting in that world of deeper feeling.

The transformative conversation that followed unfolded over several months, and I came to refer to our sessions together as 'speed bumps' for the way in which they allowed my thinking to slow down and a deeper intelligence to flow through the cracks in my much ballyhooed intellect.

For the first 40 years of my life I'd been trained to use my mind like a buzz saw, filling it up with information and cutting through the weak points in other people's arguments without ever noticing the scars I'd accumulated on my own psyche along the way. Now I began to see the value of listening without anything on my mind, allowing myself to become reflective and receptive to a wisdom that seemed to exist somewhere beyond the reach of my own experience.

ACCESSING INNATE WISDOM

Of course, once I saw the power of this deeper intelligence, the next question became how to slow down my thoughts to the point where I could actually benefit from it on a regular basis.

By this time George Pransky had become my mentor in the inside-out understanding, and he shared with me his metaphor for the workings of the mind as being like the tachometer of a racing car. Generally speaking, drivers use the tachometer to let them know when the engine is functioning optimally and when it's time to shift gear.

Now imagine that instead of measuring revolutions per minute, RPM, our mental tachometer measures thoughts per minute, or TPM.

Let's say that our brain's TPM tachometer runs on a scale something like this:

▶ *0–50 TPM*: Deeper wisdom/beautiful feelings

▶ *50–100 TPM*: Healthy functioning/good feelings

▶ *100–200 TPM*: Beginning to overload/mild stress

▶ *200–300 TPM*: Spinning out of control/persistent stress

▶ *Over 300 TPM*: Mental burnout/extreme stress

So, if we want to make the journey from stress to peace and from burnout to wisdom, we need to find a way for our thinking to slow down. We intuitively know this, which is why meditation and hypnosis have become increasingly popular in Western culture over the last 60 years and have been standard practice in Eastern and Oceanic cultures for several millennia.

The meditative state of mind is the closest thing to a 'magic wand' that I've come across in 25 years of exploring the human potential. It heals the body. It's the gateway to deeper wisdom. It opens up a world of deeper feelings. It gives us glimpses into the nature of the universe.

Most people who understand its power have learned to access it through discipline and practice over time. In fact, people put an extraordinary amount of effort into attaining and maintaining a peaceful state of mind. They try to protect their mind from disturbance by not watching the news, not reading the papers, and not allowing negative people into their life. They employ meditative techniques designed to still the mind through inquiry, mantras, and visualizations. Or they shift their attention away from their mind and onto their body, using intense exercise, gentle movement, or focusing on the breath to change their state.

Each one of these practices can be an effective way of experiencing greater peace of mind and the insights that come with it. But there's a difference between having a meditation practice and being in a meditative state of mind.

If you want to slow down your car engine, you do it by not pressing on the accelerator; if you want to slow down your thoughts, you do it by not revving them up. Which means that there's nothing you can do that will quiet the mind faster than doing nothing to quiet the mind.

And when you recognize meditation as your natural state, there's nothing you need to do to attain it. It's not only right where you are sitting now; it's the one who's doing the sitting.

MORE PERIODS, FEWER COMMAS

For a recovering intellectual who prefers to use three words when one would probably do, this has at times posed an interesting dilemma. Sometimes I still want to analyze every aspect of the universe in minute detail; at other times I just want to enjoy being alive. So I was intrigued when some friends came to visit having just returned from an 'intensive' where they'd spent several days noticing that in every single moment we're living in the feeling of our thinking.

When I asked them what they'd gotten from the experience, they reflected for a few moments, and then replied, 'More periods, fewer commas.' (Actually, they're English and they said, 'More full stops, fewer commas,' but I thought I'd translate...)

When I asked them to elaborate, they said that what they were noticing was an absence of the running commentary on experience that usually goes on in the background of the mind.

For example:

> 'I'm upset that they did that, and they need to stop, or else it means that they don't love me...'

became

> 'I'm upset.'

And

> 'I'm such an idiot, but that's judgmental, I shouldn't be so judgmental, after all, I've been learning all these wonderful things about how the mind works, and

> *I want to be a good person, but how does that work when I do something stupid, am I just supposed to sit here and not beat myself up about it and hope that I'll magically learn not to be such an idiot in the future?'*

became

> *'I'm such an idiot.'*

The resultant mental quiet they were experiencing was equivalent to having spent weeks on a meditation retreat, something both of them had done in the past as part of their search for a better and more meaningful life.

EMPTY-HEADED, FILLED WITH JOY

For some reason, the simplicity of their experience reminded me of an interview I'd once read where Oscar-winning actor Spencer Tracy was asked the secret of great acting. His response? 'Know your lines and don't bump into the furniture.'

While that remark may well have been completely tongue in cheek, it actually points to something quite fundamental about how we tend to habitually use our mind. In order to make sense of what that is, I'd like you to do a little thought experiment:

> ***Think of at least three times when you were completely lost in thought and it had outer-world consequences.***

For example, many of us get lost in thought while driving, or on a bus or train. We daydream about the future, replay conversations in our head, and generally allow our brain to take us anywhere but where we are. Most of the time we get away with it, and the disappearance of the bus, train, or motorway from our consciousness has no outer-world impact. But have you ever missed your stop, or your exit, or lost sight of the bumper of the car in front of you?

Or perhaps you were at a party or business meeting and were so caught up in your thinking that when introductions were made, you totally missed everyone's name and had to dance around it for the rest of the evening in the hope that the names would spontaneously come up again in conversation.

My own most embarrassing 'thought-full' moment was years ago when I auditioned for a play in London. The scene called for a proposal of marriage, and I took off my wedding ring to use it as a prop. I was halfway back to the train station, running through everything that had been said at the audition to see if I could figure out how well or poorly I'd done, when I realized I didn't have my ring.

I rushed back to the theater, interrupting the next actor's audition, and everyone from the director to the cleaner set about looking for my ring – until the actress I had proposed to said, 'What's that on your hand?' To my horror, my wedding ring was right where it should have been – on the ring finger of my left hand. Suffice it to say, I didn't get the part, but I've always taken some small comfort in the fact that the actor whose audition I interrupted got cast in my stead.

How about your thought-full moments? Have you ever gone looking for your glasses only to find them perched on the top of your head? Or gone in to work or school only to find it was a Saturday? Ever tried to get into the wrong car, or to fix a 'broken' piece of electrical equipment only to find it wasn't actually switched on or plugged in?

The reason everyone has at least a few of these stories in their arsenal is that we all spend an inordinate amount of time thinking about stuff. We think about what we had for dinner last night and what we're going to have for lunch today. We think about what our partner really meant when they said, 'I love you,' in a slightly distracted manner, and we think about whether we really meant it the last time we said it.

In fact, it's become so normal to always have something (or even lots of things) on our mind that we've stopped noticing how unnatural it is. After all, we weren't born with very much on our mind. But somewhere along the way, we learned to live a second life in our head. And in so doing, we began to miss out on the incredible joy, insight, richness and depth of feeling available to us in the first one.

That's not to say that thinking is bad. The capacity for critical thinking plays an important role in the evolution of our society and the development of science, mathematics, philosophy, language, and more. But if you find yourself bumping into the furniture or getting upset about the way someone you'll never meet has parked their car in a public car park, chances are your critical thinking has run amok.

In other words, Thought makes a great servant but a terrible master. Fortunately, learning to master your thinking is as simple as understanding how the mind works at a deeper level.

Imagine the mind as being a pipeline for fresh Thought, flowing straight from the deeper intelligence behind life into our consciousness, where we experience it as our personal reality. When the pipeline is open and Thought is flowing freely, our experience is fed by a gentle stream of new thoughts, insights, and creative ideas. When the pipeline is closed or clogged up with our own regurgitated thinking, we experience an endless rehash of what's already stuck inside it. Faced with this log jam of stale, repetitive thinking, we start to experience boredom, irritation, and a sense of futility and even emptiness.

If we don't understand that all that's happening is we've gotten lost in a world of our own thinking, the temptation is to 'fix' our experience by going out and creating our own best imitations of love and happiness and fulfillment. If we do understand, then we know that within moments of allowing our mind to empty and our thoughts to settle, we'll once again feel the flow of the deeper river of life.

So why is 'Know your lines and don't bump into the furniture' such great advice for life?

Because when we 'know our lines' – that is, we understand that our connection to the deeper intelligence behind the mind is continually writing the best possible script for our life – we relax into the moment and never have to worry about what we'll do or say next. And the less we have on our mind, the less likely we are to absent-mindedly bump into the furniture of our circumstances and the more effortlessly we'll navigate our life.

PUTTING IT ALL TOGETHER

Syd Banks once wrote:

> *'Let your mind be still,*
> *for the wisdom you seek is like that*
> *butterfly over yonder.*
> *If you try to catch it with*
> *your intellect,*
> *it will simply fly away.*
> *On the other hand, if you can still*
> *your mind,*
> *someday, when you least expect it,*
> *it will land in the palm of*
> *your hand.'*

As we move on to the next part of our conversation, consider taking some time off from your own thinking. Let go of all your concerns and cares for a few hours and see what comes in to fill the empty space. Worst case, you'll have a pleasant read with less background noise than you're used to. Best case, you'll get an insight into the kind of life we were all designed to live.

In the final section of the book we'll explore the implications of the inside-out understanding on performance, results, and the way we live our day-to-day lives. But before we do, here's a quick review of some insights from this chapter:

▶ When our mind is empty, it can be filled with insight from the natural intelligence that exists beyond our personal thinking. This natural intelligence is our innate wisdom.

▶ When we listen without anything on our mind, we become receptive to a wisdom that comes from beyond the reach of our own experience.

▶ Meditation – a quiet mind and a beautiful feeling – is our natural state.

▶ There's nothing we can do that will quiet the mind faster than doing nothing to quiet the mind.

▶ The less we have on our mind, the better life gets.

3

LIVING
THE DREAM

'Thought creates our world, and then says, "I didn't do it."'

David Bohm

LEARNING
HOW TO THRIVE

*'The only trick in life is to be grateful for
your highs and graceful with your lows.'*

George Pransky

For the past seven years I've hosted a weekly radio show
where people phone in for coaching on everything from
health to happiness and from starting a business to starting
a family. Newcomers to the show are often surprised that
I almost never give advice, no matter how challenging the
caller's circumstances might appear to be.

Despite this fact, callers inevitably leave the show feeling
lighter, with a greater sense of clarity about their situation
and often with the next steps of an action plan already in
place. To better understand how that works, consider the
following scenario:

You're enjoying a relaxing day in the countryside, walking along a dirt road a few miles from the nearest town, when a car comes screeching around the corner and skids to a stop, missing hitting you by inches. It's caked in mud from top to bottom, and when it stops, some of the mud comes flying off and hits you in the face.

As you wipe the grunge off your glasses, you notice that you can barely see into the car through the thick coating of mud on the windshield. Layers of glop fall to the ground as the driver rolls down his window and hurriedly apologizes, launching into a story about his wife and children being in hospital in the nearby town and his nearly drowning when he drove his car off the road and into a swamp in his haste to be at their side.

What advice would you give him?

Most people find this a fairly easy question to answer. Nearly everyone recognizes the need for this man to slow down and, at the very least, clean his windshield before making his way to town.

Many people feel compassion for him and his plight, and any hardship he nearly caused them is quickly forgotten. Some people even offer to drive him into town themselves, recognizing he's in no fit state to be doing much of anything, let alone getting back behind the wheel of a two-ton lethal missile.

What's less obvious to most people is that the exact same thing is going on in pretty much any scenario in life where we feel lost or stuck:

- We're 'driving blind,' trying to find our way forward by listening to people shouting directions at us instead of slowing down and letting the windshield of our mind clear so we can see the way forward for ourselves.

- We're 'spinning our wheels' in the mud of circumstances, alternating between trying to blast our way out by revving our engine and giving up in despair as we find ourselves stuck ever deeper in the muck.

- We're going faster and faster to meet the needs and wants of others, even when we might do irreparable damage to our body in the process.

And this is the inherent problem with even the best advice:

Until we regain our bearings, we can't use it; once we regain our bearings, we don't need it.

BEING ONLINE

Regardless of our personalities and personal histories, we all have within us a deeper essence that's untouched by conditioning and circumstances. We could call this part of us 'the light within' or 'the inner flame' and it's the source of our fundamental sense of inspiration, crackle, and aliveness. Some of my clients have called it their 'twinkle' – the spark of life inside them that appears as a twinkle in the eye on the outside.

This inner glow is made of pure Consciousness, but when we get caught up in the dream of thought, we get cut off from it. Most of us don't notice this disconnection at first, except as a vague sense of something not being quite right. Work just isn't as fulfilling as it once was, our partner isn't quite as handsome or beautiful or loving as we thought they were, and don't even get us started on what might be wrong with us...

Because we've been conditioned from birth to believe in the myth of an outside-in world, we assume the path back to well-being and joy and peace of mind must be through getting a better job or a better partner or working on becoming a better person. The irony is that the harder we work on changing ourselves in order to change the way we feel, the more distant we become from our true self, and the more important it seems to work on all those things, and the more lost we become.

So, regardless of what 'problem' we think we have, our only real problem is feeling cut off from our innate wisdom and well-being. And the moment we reconnect to that source energy, our problems stop being so problematic and we move into a new reality.

In my *Learning How to Thrive* retreats, I call this natural state of connection to the whole 'being online.' It's the space of relative clarity and well-being where we have access to both our personal database of knowledge and the deeper wisdom of Mind.

When we're online, we can be assured that whatever comes through us is likely to be of use. At these times, intuitions and insights flow through our mind like gigabytes through a data cable.

When we're offline, feeling uncomfortable, stressed, pressured, scared, or just numb, we get caught up in trying to figure things out, work them through, or overwhelm them with our brilliance.

In simple terms, being online feels better – it's that quieter, deeper feeling I've been pointing to throughout our time together. People describe it as clarity, contentment, happiness, ease, well-being, or even peace. In the quiet of that deeper feeling, we can easily hear the still small voice within. This is the way our mind is designed to work – as a clear channel to our higher wisdom.

Here's an example of how a typical day in the life might play out from these two different levels of clarity:

You wake up in the morning feeling a little bit tired. Before you leave for work, your partner reminds you in no uncertain terms that you agreed to take the kids to practice and rehearsal after school, although you're pretty sure that conversation never happened, and if it had, you would never have agreed to it in the first place.

As soon as you log on to your e-mail at work, you're faced with three urgent messages about three critical projects, each saying that strategic decisions need to be made before the end of the day if not sooner.

A quick look at your calendar shows a completely full schedule and you realize that you would need to stay at work until nearly midnight to get everything done (and that doesn't include leaving in the middle of the afternoon to drive your kids around).

How are you going to handle it?

If you act unchecked in an 'offline' state of mind, you're likely to turn each one of your daily dramas into a crisis. You and your partner will be at each other's throats over the children and you'll each be wondering how the other can be so inconsiderate. Each of your work colleagues will become the villain as you try to play the hero, working all the hours God sends to save the day while simultaneously bemoaning the fact that you're surrounded by incompetents.

Now imagine being online and living through the exact same day. You recognize that your partner's having a bad day and the impact their 'offline' state of mind is having on their communication. Their tone of voice and rolled eyes have become non-issues by the time you get to work, and you make a mental note to call them later to check in on how they're doing.

You look past the urgency in your colleagues' e-mails and see which projects really need to be acted on immediately and which will keep until the next day or even later.

Rather than try to force a decision if you don't know what to do about the kids, you put that one on the back burner, trusting that the incredible resource of innate wisdom will provide you with an answer by the time you actually need one.

And you recognize that all you can do for now is all you can do for now and don't put additional pressure or stress on yourself to play the hero and save the day.

When we're online, we see that any situation can be handled through a combination of common sense and insightful action. Any changes to be made become obvious, and while not always easy, remarkably straightforward. Life stops seeming so overwhelming, and the world stops seeming like a problem to be solved.

So how do we do it? How do we go online?

As with so many of the things we've been discussing, there's nothing to do:

Being 'online' is our natural state.

We don't need to worry about learning or practicing techniques to get or stay there, because the moment our mind clears, even if it's only for a moment, we automatically return to our factory default.

Understanding that we'll *always* get back online when our thinking slows down takes the pressure off – it's not up to us to manage our state. This allows us to take advantage of our state of mind when it's high, stay in the game when it's low, and not waste much mental or physical energy trying to change, control, or 'fix' it in between times.

Meanwhile, we'll do less damage in the world. In my experience, this is one of the most beneficial and least considered implications of the inside-out understanding – recognizing the role of Thought in creating experience makes us less inclined to run amok when we've gone offline. Instead of blaming our job, our partner, our kids, or the universe in general for our problems, we recognize that but for our thinking, we'd be having a completely different perception and experience of our situation. Consequently, there's nothing to be done other than the basics of what needs doing.

GOODWILL HUNTING

One day I was talking to a young man who'd dropped out of college as a result of a depression that had gone on for several months. He was now feeling doomed to live out the rest of his years in misery. When I asked him to catalog what had actually changed in his life during his months of malaise, he asked me what I meant.

'Well, did you drop out of school or get kicked out? That is, if you wanted to re-enroll, could you?'

He thought about it for a few moments and then acknowledged that he would be able to go back if he decided to.

'Do you still have your job?' I asked.

'For now – they've let me know they're unhappy with the drop-off in my performance, but so far they're willing to wait for me to get back on my game.'

'How about your girlfriend? Has she left you yet?' I asked, smiling.

He looked at me a bit incredulously, then smiled back. 'For some reason,' he said wryly, 'she still seems to like me.'

'Then,' I concluded, 'it seems to me that although you're a bit worse for wear, your life is still in pretty good shape.'

As he regained his bearings and found his way back online, he became more and more grateful for the fact that he hadn't done too much damage to his life while struggling with his thoughts and emotions.

****

One of the great ironies of the human condition is that we seem most motivated to make dramatic changes at precisely the moments when we're least equipped to do so. We get angry and want to change the world, but in our anger and frustration we alienate the very people who could help us to achieve our aims. Then we feel insecure and alone and think that *now* would be a good time to sort things out with our partner or children or friends.

In fact, one of the most reliable ways to spot that you've gone offline is when you feel compelled to take dramatic action to change a person, situation, or even your whole life 'once and for all.'

The truth is we all lose our bearings from time to time. We get caught up in dark thoughts or a low mood and find the world a harsh and unforgiving place. To the extent that we can see these times for what they are – momentary or even extended periods of being offline and off our game – we can limit the damage we do to our relationships, our career, and our life.

Instead of following through on the seemingly urgent directives of our own insecure thinking, we can instead step back and wait for our thoughts and feeling level to rise. Then, when we go back online and are feeling 'more ourselves,' we can once again trust our thinking, take appropriate action, and move forward.

And when we do, we thrive. We're more graceful with our lows and more grateful for our highs. And in that space of deeper understanding, we gain a deeper respect for the nature of life and the great unfolding.

PUTTING IT ALL TOGETHER

In the next chapter, we'll take a look at the deeper implications of the inside-out understanding for how we approach the game of life and the paradox of results. But before we do, here are a few of the key ideas from this section:

▶ The problem with advice is that until we regain our bearings, we can't use it; once we regain our bearings, we don't need it.

▶ We all have within us an inner flame. This is the glow of pure Consciousness.

▶ Being 'online' is our natural state.

▶ Understanding that we'll get back online the moment our thinking slows down allows us to take advantage of our state of mind when it's high, stay in the game when it's low, and not waste much mental or physical energy trying to change, manage, control, or 'fix' it in between times.

8

THE PARADOX OF RESULTS

'The great source of both the misery and disorders of human life seems to arise from overrating the difference between one permanent situation and another... Some of these situations may, no doubt, deserve to be preferred to others, but none of them can deserve to be pursued with that passionate ardor which drives us to violate the rules either of prudence or of justice, or to corrupt the future tranquility of our minds, either by shame from the remembrance of our own folly, or by remorse for the horror of our own injustice.'

Adam Smith

Before I gained some insight into the inside-out nature of experience, I used to assume that conditions and circumstances had inherent emotional feelings attached to them. Trading in volatile financial markets or working in an

ER were inherently high-pressure, high-stress jobs. Getting what you want would always make you happy. Being rich and thin meant you would be confident.

Because the creative power of Thought was largely invisible to me, I attributed my feelings (and everyone else's) to what I could see around me. And that innocent and seemingly innocuous misunderstanding is what actually lies beneath almost every problem we have in our life.

▶ Because we think our happiness comes from getting what we want, we pursue our goals at the cost of our relationships, our health, and our spiritual well-being. When we get what we want and we're still not happy, we assume the problem is that we're still not doing enough, so we push even harder and end up even further away from the experience of happiness we actually want.

▶ Because we think that our sadness comes from being on our own, we make ill-founded choices about the people we get into relationships with. Then, when we think our anger and frustration are coming from our partner, we try to change them or swap them for a different model instead of looking to Thought as the source of our experience.

▶ Because we think that our fear is causally linked to certain life circumstances, we do everything we can to avoid and/or protect ourselves from those circumstances.

Yet the moment we see that every feeling is just the shadow of a thought, we stop being scared of our feelings and just feel them.

We begin to value 'negative' feelings as much as positive ones for the insights they give us into our state of mind and how real our reality is looking to us at any given moment. And because life doesn't look so scary, we don't work so hard to make it fit the idealized pictures in our head. We relax and begin to enjoy ourselves more. We're free to express more of our natural creativity and well-being.

This is why one of the biggest shifts that people make when they begin seeing the inside-out nature of experience is from being primarily results oriented to being more inner directed. It's not that results no longer matter – it's just that those results stop validating or invalidating our value and worth in the world. Ironically, this 'take it or leave it' attitude toward results makes it easier than ever to create them.

When we take the pressure off ourselves to produce results at any cost, and instead rest in our innate well-being, enjoying our life, following our wisdom, and looking within for a deeper understanding of how it all works, things often seems to unfold more beautifully than we could ever have imagined. We start to notice all sorts of synchronicities and serendipities, and outcomes that may have eluded us for years begin to happen seemingly 'all by themselves.'

Yet the moment the results we've been waiting for start to show up, we become tempted to throw ourselves right back into the outside-in, action-oriented paradigm that makes creating specific results seem to matter more than our overall experience of being alive. If we succumb to the illusion, we take ourselves out of the foundational, formless space from which those results have been effortlessly created.

And this raises a very interesting question:

In a world where getting what we want may or may not lead to happiness, losing the big game doesn't have to hurt, and other people don't have the power to make us happy or miserable (even if they're related to us), how do we know what course to set in life?

Since 'there' isn't inherently better than 'here,' the direction we head in becomes almost as arbitrary as how long we give ourselves to get there.

Similarly, the idea of putting pressure on ourselves to strive for our goals now so that we can feel the rush of reaching them later is as bizarre and misguided a life strategy as hitting ourselves in the face because it feels good when we stop.

This points to what is perhaps our society's most unproductive and ill-founded bias: the notion that happiness can only come via success and at the cost of struggle, stress, and sacrifice.

In other words, according to this poorly conceived mathematical equation:

Struggle + Stress + Sacrifice = Success = Happiness

or, to simplify it even further:

Unhappiness = Success = Happiness

which ultimately leaves us with the oxymoronic formula:

Unhappiness = Happiness

But when we begin to see that we're the ones making up the conditions for our own success and happiness and then doing our best to fulfill them, it opens up the possibility of playing the game in a brand new way.

A WHOLE NEW WAY OF BEING IN THE WORLD

When our kids were younger, Nina and I would enjoy going along to watch them compete in everything from baseball games to sack races at the school fair. The reason we enjoyed the competition was because it really didn't matter to us whether our kids did well or poorly or whether they won or lost. When they did well, we would go, 'Yaaaay –

let's go get some ice cream!' If they did poorly, we would say, 'Awwwww – let's go get some ice cream!'

One of the most significant implications of the inside-out understanding is that but for our thinking, there's no challenge in life that couldn't be met with the same level of joyful indifference. And contrary to our cultural expectation, that lack of self-generated pressure frees us up to perform at our best and enjoy the game fully.

Imagine the following scenario:

> *You're offered a job working at a casino. In order to encourage other people to play, you're paid $500 a night to gamble with the house's money. You're given $50,000 in chips at the start of the evening; at the end of the night, you turn in whatever chips you have left and leave with your $500 in your pocket.*

What would that actually be like? Chances are if you were able to quadruple your money you'd be excited at the time, but at the end of the night, after turning in your chips, you'd forget all about it. Similarly, if you lost it all, you'd likely be disappointed – until you remembered that it was all just a game and the real payoff was already in your pocket. You'd play full out and fearless both because you had nothing at stake and because it would be obvious to you that, as with most things in life, it isn't actually up to you how things turn out. The fact is, some stuff just isn't in the cards – for now. Sometimes you win, sometimes you lose. That's what makes it a game.

What would it be like to play the game of life with that same degree of fearlessness and freedom, knowing that everything that really counted – your well-being, happiness, love, and self-worth – was already yours to keep? After all, you were born with them, and the only thing that can ever take you away from them is a thought. You can get nothing of true and lasting value from playing the game of life that wasn't already yours before you started playing and won't continue to be yours after the game is done.

At this point, we're no longer playing to win – in the divine dream of life, the only possible reason to play is to play. If you've ever seen a five year old playing a game of make-believe, you know they throw themselves into it as if their lives depended on it because they know full well that their lives don't. The same is true for us.

Except on those extremely rare occasions when our life (as opposed to our livelihood) might actually be on the line, we're playing with the house's money. Contrary to the way it appears from time to time in the illusion of our thinking, there's nothing real at stake. And the only thing we have to lose is the illusion that something outside us can make us happy, safe, and secure.

For myself, I've found that the rewards of an inner-directed life lived (mostly) from a place of well-being far outweigh the short-term gains of a 'results at any cost' mentality. Either I have a wonderful life and drive a Porsche or I have a wonderful life and ride a bicycle – either way, I keep showing up each day and playing. Because being alive is the best game in town.

HUMILITY MADE FUN

One day I was sitting with a client who was telling me about his business struggles, and how the stress and pressure he was feeling were leaking into other areas of his life. Out of nowhere, a question that at first seemed too rude to voice popped into my head: *'Why aren't you awesomer?'*

It was such a direct question that it made me smile, and when my client asked me what I was smiling about I told him and he asked me what I meant.

'I'm not sure,' I confessed, 'but I think what I mean is this: you're a very successful guy, so I know you're at the very least capable of hard work and delivering on what you promise. You're well educated, so I know your brain works just fine, and I've been around you long enough to know you're socially intelligent as well. But somehow you're acting as though you no longer have access to the same resources that have gotten you this far in life. And I don't mind, but it's curious to me…'

We both sat with that thought for awhile, and he shared some of the doubts that had crept into his mind as he'd struggled to keep his business afloat over the past couple of years – thoughts like *What if my success was just a fluke? and What if my time has passed?*

Rather than address those questions directly, I took us back into a conversation about the *nature* of the human experience. We talked about the nature of Thought, and how everyone experiences their thinking as though it's real. This took us into a contemplation of the formless energy out of which thought and every form arises and dissipates, and we both got pretty quiet.

Finally, he asked me, 'Why do you think I'm not awesomer?'

I reflected for a few moments, and then shared what came to me.

'I think it's because somewhere along the line, how you were doing in life started to seem very real and significant, and that was a scary thought, as it would be for anyone. And because it looked so real and important, you started to think that you needed things to be a certain way in order to manage your fear. And if all your attention is focused on trying to control the world, it's really difficult to stay tuned in to your deeper guidance and wisdom, which is where all our "awesomeness" comes from in the first place.'

I shared with my client that life had been kicking my ass a bit over the previous few weeks. It was nothing major and nothing irreversible, but some things I'd thought were done had come undone and I'd suffered through a couple of days of self-pity before recognizing that I was a bit out of touch with reality.

Things had been going so well for so long that I'd forgotten how little control I actually had over how they turned out. Without even noticing, I'd begun to accept good things happening as my birthright and to expect deferential treatment from a universe that might not even have known I existed. I found the reality check quite refreshing.

At that point, something that Syd Banks once said about humility came to mind:

> *'Humility isn't thinking less of yourself;*
> *it's thinking of yourself less.'*

In this sense, humility *is* humanity. It's nothing to do with high or low self-esteem; it's about recognizing the fact that we're one of six billion waves in the ocean of life, each no more or less important than any other.

Without my having to do anything about it, the sun comes up in the morning and the stars twinkle at night. Before I've even gotten out of bed, the Earth has spun a third of the way round its axis and six billion people have done the best they know to do to increase their happiness and mitigate their suffering.

And since I'm not in charge, I get to relax and enjoy the ride. Rather than cower in recognition of my own weakness and even helplessness in the face of forces far greater than my own, I'm set free. Free to appreciate my life when things are going my way and to handle them with grace when they're not. Free to love and contribute to people when they behave the way I want them to and to continue to love and contribute to them when they don't. Free to go out and create the life I want when things seem easy and free and to continue to move in that direction or even give up and go back to the drawing board when they seem hard.

And in the end, that seems to me to be the core of all our desires: the freedom to be able to enjoy our life and be a contribution to the whole in sickness and in health, for richer or for poorer, as best we can for as long as we're here. How things ultimately turn out isn't up to us. It never was. But if we do our bit and play our part, it's remarkable how far we can go.

I shared all this with my client and then we sat in silence for awhile, enjoying the deeper feeling that comes when contemplating the deeper nature of life.

'That's pretty awesome,' he said.

And I had to agree that it was.

PUTTING IT ALL TOGETHER

In our final chapter together, we'll explore the far side of empowerment and take a walk along the path of the soul. In the meantime, here are a few of the key ideas from this chapter:

- The moment we see that every feeling is just the shadow of a thought, we stop being scared of our feelings and just feel them.

- We're playing with the house's money. There's nothing real at stake. The only thing we have to lose is the illusion that something outside us can make us happy, safe, and secure.

- When you're playing to play, being alive is the best game in town.

- Humility isn't thinking less of yourself; it's thinking of yourself less.

- How things ultimately turn out isn't up to us. It never was. But if we do our bit and play our part, it's remarkable how far we can go.

9

BEYOND EMPOWERMENT

'Our free will can hinder the course of inspiration, and when the favourable gale of God's grace swells the sails of our soul, it is in our power to refuse consent and thereby hinder the effect of the wind's favour; but when our spirit sails along and makes its voyage prosperously, it is not we who make the gale of inspiration blow for us, nor we who make our sails swell with it, nor we who give motion to the ship of our heart; but we simply receive the gale, consent to its motion and let our ship sail under it, not hindering it by our resistance.'

St. François de Sales

I was speaking with a client once who was very concerned about what she described as her inability to 'access God's wisdom' while working through a variety of challenges in her business and personal life. She told me that she had a bumper sticker on her car that read 'God is my Co-pilot' and that she always turned to a higher power for support. Most of the time, she felt incredibly supported. But in times of real need and crisis, she struggled to feel that connection or hear the guidance.

So we talked about how when we get caught up in the machinations of the intellect it becomes considerably more difficult to hear the whispers of a deeper intelligence.

I shared the story of a comedian who'd called me in for 'emergency coaching' before his first gig in front of thousands of people. While I knew he was hoping for some emotional management tools around confidence and charisma, what wound up resolving the situation for him was when I pointed out that his own thoughts about it being a 'really big gig' were the only things standing in the way of his natural confidence and charisma.

My client and I then went on to talk about the difference between trying to use guidance to fulfill your personal goals and allowing yourself to be guided to fulfill your role in the unfolding of life. We both enjoyed exploring the difference between chasing after the whims and desires of the personality and being guided by the inspiration of the soul.

It reminded me of one of my favorite stories about Abraham Lincoln, first recounted in the sermon delivered at his funeral and no doubt distorted in the retelling over the years. At the height of the American Civil War, when things were looking bleak for the Union, one of Lincoln's generals concluded a battle planning meeting by saying, 'Let us hope that God is on our side!'

Lincoln apparently responded with great feeling, 'No, General, let us hope that *we* are on *God's* side.'

This took us back to some of the fundamental questions about the nature of the human experience we've been exploring in this book:

▶ How much influence do we actually have over our own life?

▶ Does free will mean that we're responsible for everything that happens to us, or does it only extend as far as our responses and reactions to what happens?

▶ How do we know that we're playing our part in the great unfolding of life?

These are questions for the ages, and while I lay no great claim to the 'right' answers, I did suggest to my client that she might consider getting a new bumper sticker, one that read 'I am God's Co-pilot.'

A few weeks later I was teaching a coaching program and one of the students, an officer candidate in the armed forces, was expressing his concern that despite his considerable efforts, at the age of 22 he had not yet become the man he wanted to be or changed the world in the way he thought it ought to be changed. Each attempt I made to point out how well it seemed to me that he was doing was doggedly argued with evidence that proved only how high he'd set the bar.

I finally abandoned my perhaps misguided attempts at reassurance and pointed out the deeper truth. 'You're not the pilot on this mission,' I said. 'You're the plane.'

THE PATH OF THE SOUL

I spent the first 25 years or so of my life as a reasonably successful victim. At times, the apparent unfairness of life would get me down, and I nearly drowned in a sea of what I now know to have been dodgy brain chemistry. As I slowly got my bearings, I did my best to fight back against the victim voice inside my head with a cacophony of plans and schemes designed not so much to create things in the world as to take me away from my own unhappiness and insecurity.

Some of those plans and schemes actually worked out, and in spite of my own worst efforts I met the girl of my dreams, got a job on a television sitcom in Wales, and learned that sometimes a can-do attitude actually can pay off.

I began to study the personal empowerment and success literature in earnest, and for the next ten years or so I set higher and higher goals and even achieved some of them. Sure, I was stressed as hell, but I'd learned to 'man up,' broaden my shoulders and take it.

To better understand this path, imagine a continuum going from left to right:

HELPLESS ⬅━━━━━━━━━➡ **EMPOWERED**

On the left-hand side of the continuum we see ourselves as helpless victims of circumstance. There's not much point in setting a direction in life because we believe that we have no choice about what to do – we have to stay married or get divorced, keep working at the same dead-end job or leave immediately, allow ourselves to be bullied or 'defend our honor' by fighting back at every imagined slight.

But as we become more conscious of our role in creating our experience of life, we realize that we aren't really helpless victims and we begin to see that even in the direst circumstances we do have some choices, although we may not particularly like any of the ones we're currently able to see.

The further we go toward the right of the continuum, the more empowered we feel and the more choices we become aware of until we realize that in any situation we have a nearly infinite range of choices. There are not only innumerable actions we could take (though some of them may take great courage), but we also have choices about our attitude and the meaning we ascribe to whatever it is that's happening.

This would seem to be the pinnacle of possibility on the empowered path of life:

HELPLESS ←――――――→ EMPOWERED

Victim	*Creator*
Fear	*Courage*
No Choice	*Choice*

Compared with the quiet desperation of being a victim, the testosterone surge of empowerment felt amazing. I set my direction, planned my work, and worked my plan. Yet in the back of my mind I knew something was off. I was beginning to meet with some extraordinarily successful people. Many of them were just like me – happy and confident when things were going well; petty and desperate when they weren't. We wore masks of arrogance or indifference to hide a head full of insecurity and fear.

But some people I met seemed to be on a different path, even though they had many of the same things that I was working so hard to achieve. As I looked to see what was different about them, I realized they were following inner wisdom instead of outer goals. They still wound up getting somewhere in the game of life. It's just that it didn't matter so much to them where that happened to be.

Instead of striving to be the predominant creative force in their life themselves, they delighted in being conduits for a creative force – the principle of Mind – that existed far beyond the consciousness of the fragile ego-mind. In short, they allowed their life to unfold from a place of connection with a deeper wisdom that seems to be an innate part of the human potential.

This opened up a new possibility for how to live in the world:

HELPLESS ←——→ EMPOWERED ←——→ ENLIGHTENED

Victim	*Creator*	*Conduit*
Fear	*Courage*	*Insight*
No Choice	*Choice*	*No Choice*

I call this enlightened approach 'the path of the soul' because I've observed that the moment someone begins to follow their inner promptings and live insightfully in the moment, their life begins to unfold with a beauty and perfection that their own best-laid plans never seemed to have. It's as if their own soul is designing the perfect path and laying it out in front of them, one daily brick at a time.

When we begin to see the illusion of our thinking more clearly, we realize that in a world where our experience is being created from the inside out, mastering the circumstances of our life is the booby prize. That doesn't mean we might not wind up with a big house or a nice car – there's nothing wrong with tapping into the abundance of the universe if the opportunity comes our way. It's just that we're unlikely to spend too much time chasing the dream of success when we're awake to the dream of life.

Once we start to recognize the feeling of our innate wisdom, we realize that when it comes to setting our direction in life, we don't really have that much of a choice after all. This isn't because we've gone back to being victims, but rather because we're pretty much always going to go where that inner wisdom directs us. Not because we 'have to,' but because not going where the intelligence behind life wants to take us would be self-defeating and a little bit silly.

To highlight the difference between trying to make things happen as a self-empowered individual and opening up to the creative guidance of Mind as a part of the great unfolding, consider the analogy of a sailboat. Trying to 'make things happen' in your life is like trying to make the boat move forward by blowing into the sails. It's not that you can't get anywhere – it's that you tend to exhaust yourself in the process and miss out on a lot of what's going on outside your boat.

By way of contrast, allowing the energy of life to guide you is like allowing the wind to fill your sails and propel you forward. If you've ever had the feeling of something coming 'through' you instead of 'from' you, you know what the wind feels like. We experience it as inspiration, or flow, or being in the zone. We make more progress in a few hours of inspired action than we did in months of hard work and struggle.

A friend of mine who spent many years as a priest before turning his hand to a different kind of spiritual teaching shared a similar analogy with me:

'No matter how hard a surfer works,
the ocean is doing most of the heavy lifting.'

And this, for me, is the limitation of the empowered approach to life. Empowerment asks us to be a 'force of nature,' not recognizing that the operant power behind any force of nature is nature itself. This is the essence of the path of the soul:

When you allow a deeper wisdom to come through you, that deeper wisdom inevitably comes through.

THE REPAIR OF THE WORLD

One of my favorite teaching stories comes from the world of Jewish mysticism:

In the beginning, there was only God. But God decided to create the world by withdrawing his divine light and pouring it in to specially prepared vessels.

Unfortunately, as God poured his light into the vessels, they shattered, sending sparks of God's divine light and shards of the vessels to every corner of creation.

> *Our great task is to assist God by gathering the divine sparks back together and restoring the vessel to wholeness. Until all the sparks of God's light are gathered back together, the work of creation will not be complete. This task is called 'Tikun Olam' – the repair of the world.*

I've realized that this is what I love doing – finding the spark of divine light inside people, fanning that spark, and watching and witnessing as their lives burst into flame. This inner spark is our essential nature and, as Syd Banks pointed out repeatedly, it's never more than one thought away.

For everything that I don't know about the world, there are a few things that I do, and first and foremost amongst these is that the divine light is always shining inside us and its warmth is in the feeling, not the words.

We can get so caught up in trying to remember to live by the wisdom and insights of others that we forget the source of that wisdom is inside us as well. Insights are a part of the factory default, the natural side-effects of living with a relatively quiet mind and a relatively beautiful feeling. If you forget everything we've talked about in this conversation but you stay with the feeling, the insights will continue to unfold for you.

And while the inside-out unfolding of the path of the soul is certainly less predictable than the outside-in architecture of the empowered one, it is, in my experience so far, the path most in line with the kindness of the design.

EPILOGUE:
THE LIFE COACH AND
THE MIGHTY TREE

*'What you leave behind is not what
is engraved in stone monuments, but
what is woven into the lives of others.'*

Pericles

One day, while sitting with my back against the trunk of a massive tree in my garden, I fell asleep and dreamed that I was sitting with my back against the trunk of a massive tree in my garden. Much to my surprise, it asked me for some coaching.

'I am a mighty tree,' it began, 'and I'm somewhat embarrassed to admit that a few of my leaves have begun to fall to the ground. The thing is, I can't afford to lose my leaves. What will people think of me if I go bald? They'll see me as naked and weak and frail. I'm not sure I can go on if it means going through such a difficult ordeal.'

'But, tree,' I replied, 'surely you must realize that this is just a part of the seasons of life. Each autumn you lose your leaves – that's why we humans call it "fall." And come spring you'll grow new leaves and return more beautiful than ever.'

'How can you say such things with such certainty?' said the tree (who obviously hadn't read my books). 'Are you some kind of psychic or fortune-teller?'

'No, tree, I'm not psychic – I'm simply an observer of life. And I've noticed the natural cycle that all trees of your kind go through. In fact, everywhere I look in nature I see the same kind of pre-existing intelligence at work behind the scenes.'

'You're not talking about God, are you?' asked the tree. 'I'm not sure that I want to get into a discussion about God with a human.'

'Neither do I, tree – neither do I. When I say "pre-existing intelligence," I mean the implicate order of things. As you know, acorns never grow into pine trees and baby rabbits never grow up to be grizzly bears. Somehow, the fruit is already programmed into the seed. We humans can observe that intelligence at work in our body. The moment we get cut, the intelligence of the body begins the process of healing. Everything the body does is designed to return itself to a state of natural health and equilibrium. There's an intelligence behind our mind as well. The moment we think a toxic thought, we get a toxic feeling as a warning signal not to proceed too far down that path. Healthy thoughts produce healthy feelings, letting us know that we're heading in a healthy direction. This inner compass guides us back to a state of natural mental health and equilibrium. In this state, we have access to an otherwise hidden wisdom that will guide us if we let it.'

'Then why is there so much war, and cruelty, and unrest in your world?' the tree asked. 'Surely that's proof that no such wisdom exists.'

'Unfortunately, not everyone yet understands the inside-out nature of reality and the simple intelligence behind the system, so there's still a lot of mental instability in the world. But it seems to me the fact that no matter how long people have suffered they're never more than one thought away from peace is proof of the kindness of the design.'

The tree stared down at me inscrutably, as if it could hold its pose for a thousand years without wavering. Finally, it spoke.

'But even if this wisdom and intelligence exists, it is not infallible. Humans die, and so do trees. If there is, as you say, a "kindness to the design," how do you explain death?'

It was my turn to stare back up at the tree.

'I can't explain it,' I responded honestly. 'But I can observe it and see the impersonal nature of it. And somehow seeing that it's a part of the natural cycle for everyone and everything suggests to me that even death, at some level that I can't yet see, is a part of the implicate order. Perhaps in some way it's even a part of the kindness of the design.'

We sat quietly together, the tree and I, feeling connected not only by my back against its trunk but by a deeper bond of shared contemplation and mortality.

Our conversation is ongoing. The more I look in this direction, the more I realize how little I see. But somehow, the little I see makes my life better and better...

With all my love,

RESOURCES

As is always the case when a revolution takes hold in any field, the number of available resources increases at an exponential rate. While I will share many of the resources I found most helpful in my own research and immersion below, for a more comprehensive and up-to-date list you can visit: www.supercoach.com/ior/resources

SYD BANKS

Syd's books, audios, and videos are deceptively simple (or deceptively complex, depending on your state of mind when you first encounter them). Consequently, I recommend going through them multiple times. With the exception of *The Missing Link*, all of his books are written in parable form.

Books

Second Chance

In Quest of the Pearl

The Missing Link: Reflections on Philosophy and Spirit

The Enlightened Gardener: A Novel

The Enlightened Gardener Revisited: A Wise Old Gardener Teaches Life's Principles of Mind, Consciousness, and Thought

Dear Liza

Audio

Attitude: Using the Three Principles to Deal with Stress & Insecurity

The Great Spirit: Reflections on North American Spirituality

One Thought Away: Syd Banks at Tampa Crossroads

What is Truth?

DVD

The Hawaii Lectures: Secret to the Mind; Oneness of Life; The Power of Thought; Going Home

The Long Beach Lectures: The Great Illusion; Truth Lies Within; The Experience; Jumping the Boundaries

The Washington Lectures: The Three Principles; Separate Realities

While Syd died in 2009, his website (www.sydneybanks.org) has been maintained and contains some short video clips and further information about his materials.

GEORGE PRANSKY

Much of George's work was only available to private clients until recently, but he has produced dozens of audios covering a vast array of applications. I've listened to and enjoyed all of them – I've listed a small sampling of my favorites below:

Books

The Relationship Handbook: A Simple Guide to Satisfying Relationships

The Renaissance of Psychology (currently out of print)

Audio

Busy Mind: How Your Mental Speed Affects Your Life

The Game of Life and Living: The Interface of Inner Calm and Outer World Achievement

Investment vs. Involvement: Two Independent Aspects of Life

Leveraging the Human Dimension in Business: Discover the Most Important Variable In Human Performance

Maintenance-Free Relationships: How to Improve Your Relationship without 'Working on it'

Some Fun, No Fun, All Fun: The Key to Unlocking Your Enjoyment in Life

You can find all of George's products along with a number of new programs featuring his wife, Linda, and his daughters, Kara and Erika, at www.pranskyandassociates.com

MICHAEL NEILL

I offer a number of ways to go deeper in the inside-out understanding, including one-on-one coaching, mentoring and supervision, multimedia programs, small group retreats, and an international certification-based coaching program.

For a full listing of our current offerings, please visit www.supercoach.com

If you are interested in professional training, please visit www.supercoachacademy.com

ADDITIONAL RESOURCES

Books

Every few months, new books come out that address some aspect of the three principles and the inside-out understanding. As well as those by Syd and George, the ones I find myself recommending most often include:

Clarity: Clear Mind, Better Performance, Bigger Results, Jamie Smart (Capstone, 2013)

Our True Identity... Three Principles, Elsie Spittle (CreateSpace Independent Publishing Platform, 2010)

Somebody Should Have Told Us!: Simple Truths for Living Well, Jack Pransky (CCB Publishing, 2011)

Stillpower: Excellence with Ease in Sports and Life, Garret Kramer (Beyond Words Publishing, 2012)

The Wisdom Within, by Roger Mills and Elsie Spittle (Lone Pine Publishing, 2001)

Websites

Here are three of the most active sites currently operating as portals to The Three Principles community:

www.threeprinciplesmovies.com
A fantastic resource packed with hundreds of video interviews with most of the major teachers and practitioners from around the world.

www.3PGC.com
A non-profit organization committed to bringing an understanding of The Three Principles to people throughout the world, offering blogs and webinars from a variety of teachers.

www.tikun.co.uk
A Jewish organization that has done a phenomenal job of making The Three Principles available to people from all walks of life and inclusive of all faiths and backgrounds.

ACKNOWLEDGMENTS

Writing a book is somewhat uniquely both a completely solitary endeavor and something that's utterly impossible without a great team around you. To write this book in particular, I had to first give myself permission to upset a number of people I care about in order to ensure the words came through 'clean,' untainted by my unenlightened desire to please everyone and offend no-one. However, after the manuscript was written, I gave it to six people whose opinions I value and trust – an engineer, a spiritual teacher, a businessman, a psychiatrist, a psychologist, and an editor. My deepest gratitude to David Glazer, Clarence Thomson, Don Donovan, Dr. Bill Pettit, Dr. George Pransky, and Lizzie Hutchins. Without their direct, honest, and wildly varied feedback, the book you've just read would have been a very different creature indeed.

I'd like to acknowledge everyone who has taken the time to teach, coach, and mentor me in deepening my understanding of the inside-out paradigm over the past six years, including Joseph Bailey, Dicken Bettinger, Keith Blevens, Cheryl Bond, Cathy Casey, Robin Charbit, Chip Chipman, Jan Chipman, Don Donovan, Mara Gleason, Mark Howard, Robert Kausen, Sandy Krot, Ken Manning, Kristen Mansheim, Gabriela Maldonado-Montano, Leslie Miller, Ami Mills-Naim, Valda Monroe, Jack Pransky, Linda Pransky, Bill Pettit, Judith Sedgeman, Elsie Spittle, and Aaron Turner.

Extra special thanks to Syd Banks, whose insights opened up a new world to me, and George Pransky, for inspiring my journey and then becoming my guide, friend, and mentor along the way.

To translate ideas and insights into a book that goes out into the world takes a team, and I have been blessed with a mighty one:

▶ Terri Carey and Joe Alamo, the magical elves who take my mad ramblings each week and turn them into tips, web pages, and programs while I sleep. Without you, I wouldn't even attempt to do the work I do.

▶ Robert Kirby, my amazing agent, who teased the idea for this book out of my head over a glass of whiskey and a wonderful meal.

▶ Lizzie Hutchins, my intrepid editor, who took a month and a half to pay me a compliment without ever letting me doubt that she was firmly on my side.

▶ Michelle Pilley, Margarete Nielsen, and Reid Tracy, whose belief in me never wavered even when my belief in myself was riding the rollercoaster of thought.

▶ The amazing editorial and support team at Hay House, with special thanks to Amy Kiberd, Julie Oughton, Ruth Tewkesbury, and Steve Williams.

▶ Randy Stuart, a designer who appeared in my life out of nowhere and delivered exactly what was needed. That's what angels do – just saying!

My clients, readers, listeners, and students have in many ways been my best teachers, helping me to hone my expression of these principles into something that can be understood and grasped at deeper and deeper levels. My gratitude to all, with special mention to loyal readers of the weekly tips (12 years and going strong!), avid listeners of Hay House Radio, students of Supercoach Academy, and those who've allowed me to mentor them over the past 5 years, including Ali Campbell, Elese Coit, Maggie Gilewicz, Anders Haglund, Fiona Jacob, Martin Jarnland, Kajen Kanagasabai, Rich Litvin, Bevin Lynch, Toni McGuinness, Donald McNaughton, Susan Motheral, Richard Nugent, Barb Patterson, Claire Shutes, Jamie Smart, Jayne Styles, and Sue Trinder.

I decided years ago that if I had to choose, I would sacrifice business success for friends and family, and it's a credit to my friends and family that I've never had to make that choice. All my love and thanks to:

▶ David Beeler – my best friend for over 25 years. We've walked more than 10,000 miles together (literally) and you've always been the first to sign up to play guinea pig to whatever mad experiment or new idea I want to try out.

▶ Paul McKenna – my other brother. You've made the journey more fun than I had any right to expect or hope for.

▶ Oliver, Clara, and Maisy – the best children in the world. Spending time with you is like having a cuddle with God.

▶ And last, but by no means least, to Nina – no matter how many times I disappear into my head, you are always waiting for me when I re-emerge. I am truly blessed to have you as my wife.

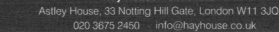

ABOUT THE AUTHOR

Photographer: David Beeler

Michael Neill is an internationally renowned transformative coach and the bestselling author of *You Can Have What You Want, Supercoach, Feel Happy Now!,* and both the *Effortless Success* and *Coaching from the Inside-Out* audio programs. He has spent the past 23 years as a coach, adviser, friend, mentor, and creative spark plug to celebrities, CEOs, royalty, and people who want to get more out of themselves and their lives. He is the also the founder of **Supercoach Academy**, an international school that teaches people how to coach from the inside out.

Michael's books have been translated into 13 languages, and his public talks, retreats, and seminars have touched and transformed lives at the United Nations and on five continents around the world. He hosts a weekly talk show on HayHouseRadio.com, and his weekly blogs can be read on his website and *The Huffington Post.*

You can follow him on Facebook and Twitter:

 www.facebook.com/mneill

www.twitter.com/michael_neill